Sorcery (magic)
Made Man
To leave Eden

This letter of Akini is a sign of the love of.God for witches, magicians, witch doctors, those who practice the forbidden etc ... GOD opens his hands to receive them in his kingdom of love.

I also love you and my heart desires to see you into the kingdom of love.

The author Akini Tenzapa Dieudonne reserves the right on the book. The Book is released by www.ingramspark.com and available on www.amazon.com market places.

Person is authorized to copy this book for commerce. Buy a copy and keep it in your heart!

Author: PASTOR AKINI TENZAPA DIEUDONNE
Title: "Sorcery (magic)
　　　　Made man
　　　　　To leave Eden "

© 2016 AKINI DIEUDONNE
facebook.com/TenzapaAkini
Twitter.com/TenzapaAkini
Or like my page fcb/TenzapaAkiniHouse
akin@webmail.co.za

AKINI-TENZAPA DIEUDONNE was born on 28.mai.1979 and called to serve the Lord Jesus Christ by the will of the living God. To all who are in Christ, to those who behave according to the course of this world, those who pray statues, to those who serve Satan by conscience and ignorance, may the Grace of God who made all things, the world and all that it contains, may God who made the angels and angels who rebelled with Satan, demons, may God who lives forever and ever be with your hearts!

The letter of akini is not writen to judge but to bring the true light that comes from one who created us according to their image and their likeness.

The creator God loves everyone:
Africans, Europeans, American, Oceans, Asians! He sends rain on the good and the bad.

Reading the entire letter of akini Volume 2 will open your eyes to discover the will of him who crushes the devil, satan forever and ever!

The letter of akini v2 will also help you to get some knowledge:

1. How can you resist the devil!

2. 3 temptations of the devil!
3. the impact of the prayer that the Lord Jesus has
   Shown us!
4. The real reason that pushed GOD
   to give Abraham a land belonging
   To other Nations!
5. Is it a sin to drink alcohol?
6. Why does Christmas exist
7. Can we pray God in the form
   of image?
8 Africans, Europeans, Americans
   Ocean, and throughout Asia, can they
   Inherit the blessing of Abraham, Isaac
   And Jacob
9. Being Jewish is it an assurance for salvation
   In the eyes of God of Abraham, Isaac, and Jacob?

10. The ceremonies of law, are they Abolished?
11. circumcision which gives salvation!
12. the impact of the meal of the Lord
13. the impact of the body of the Lord Jesus Christ!
14. the impact of the blood of the Lord Jesus Christ!
15. the true baptism of water!
16 the impact of the baptism of spirit!
17. the impact of the baptism of fire!
18. the impact of fire!
19. how to operate deliverance of Sorcerers, magicians, witchdoctors, those who practice taboos, "
    "How to perform the resurrection of a dead person"
20 .You will also know AKINI-DIEUDONNE

You will discover many other things!

The content of the letter of akini volume 2, are words that the living God has put into the mouth of his servant AKINI DIEUDONNE to write.

Those who believe that The Holy Spirit speaks to men also believe in the letter of Akini "Sorcery (magic)
                    Made man
                        To leave Eden "
Use the Holy Bible to check the accounts mentioned !

Also learn that "The speech of Akini"
Will be published at its time:

  "We are like
     God for
  Knowledge of life"

Do not miss it too! God has always acted more than before! I mean that the Holy Spirit will speak other things that you did not hear!

Let us hold hands and say:

Our Father who is in heaven! May your name be sanctify , let your kingdom come, let your will be done on earth as in heaven. Amen!

Volume 2 is the development of the first letter of Akini:
"sorcery (magic)
   Made man
     To leave Eden "

Before speaking of volume 2, I would like first to repete the first letter of Akini:
               "Sorcery (magic)
                Made man
                To leave Eden "

Several reasons have been advanced why God drove man and his wife out of the garden, but I want all of us to analyze in the Bible which actually happened into the garden.

Genese3-:4-5. Then the serpent said to the woman you
shall not die, but God knows that the day you
 will eat your eyes will open and you
Shall be as gods knowing good and evil.

The snake in question is the devil (satan). Revelation 12:9. In his words we see that the devil was offering to the woman a power which was not from God and a power that is not from God is automatically from devil (Satan), and as we know we have two masters: God and Satan

Brother (sister) a sorcerer or magician has power like gods!

 Sorcery, magic, fetishism, etc. ... these are just names of the power of Satan!

GENESIS 3:7 - The eyes of the one and the other opened in the words of the serpent!

GENESIS 3:22, GOD has recognized that man had another power in him (the evil power) because he said: Here the man is become as one of us to the knowledge of good and evil.

And now, let prevent him to put his hand and take the tree of live to eat and live forever.

Here we clearly see that man was separated from God because he had a new power in him what I call the power of the devil (sorcery, magic, etc. ..)

WHY DOES GOD PLACED THE TREE OF KNOWLEDGE OF GOOD AND EVIL IN THE GARDEN?

Brother (sr) this was not the will of God to put the tree in the garden because God is love and not tempt man. Jacques 1:13

The idea came from the devil because is the accusator. 1 Thessalonians 3:5

The devil often time stands before God for permission to tempt the children of God.
Job 1:6-12 Job 2:1-7

Brother (sr), we are at the time whereby satan urge his power into the world: sorcery, magic, etc ...

Brother (sr), we are living the fulfillment of Revelation 13:16-18, where according to the plan of the devil you must belong to an occult science for progress, success. In fact every person belonging to an occult science (framasson, maicari, Rosicrucian, etc ...) receives a registered number666 which gives access to the wealth of the world.

Brother (sr) the devil is sharing sorcery, magic .. by force to men, that is why we must rise ingront of the whole world to teach men and women to worship the one true Living God creator of heaven and earth and the alpha and omega , eternal where does come Christ Jesus the saviour of the world

WHY GOD IS AGAINST SORCERY (MAGIC)?

God is against magic (sorcery) because it brings man to think only of evil against his neighbor and to live in abomination before God.

Brother (sr) you who serve Satan by sorcery, magic, occult science, etc ... know that you are in a big mistake because In the devil there is no love.

Listen! The devil makes you rich not because he loves you but he wants you to be destroyed with him at Judgement Day. Revelation 20:7-10. Revelation 20:11-15

My brother! I want you to choose between God and Satan, and I would like your conscience to respond to the following question:

WHO IS GOOD BETWEEN GOD AND SATAN?

-God said you shall not kill, but satan asks you to kill your brother or your mother or your sister or your child for the promotion, success, wealth etc ...

-God said you shall not commit adultery but the devil leads you to commit it with a girl of 7 years-10 years for promotion, success, fortune, etc. ..

-God said you shall not uncover the nakedness of your father, your mother, your brother, your sister, your uncle, your child, aunt, but the devil asks you to do it for promotion, success, fortune etc. ..

-God said you shall not sleep with a man as one sleep with a woman but the devil asks you for promotion, success, wealth, etc. .. Leviticus 18:2

-God said you shall not sleep with a beast but the devil asks you to do it for power, domination, success,etc.. Leviticus6:23

God told man to be fruitful and multiply but the devil asks him to destroy its fruitfulness for wealth, success, power, promotion etc...

Just with the above: who is right between God and Satan?

I, AKINI-DIEUDONNE, I prefer GOD for his commandments are better and full of love.

My brother, my sister, I' d like you to complete the sentence below!

By supplementing you declare before God and Satan, who is your Master .MATTHEW 6:24

NB: Do not fill the other sheet, maybe you can have a good heart to multiply these leaves.
"I, ..., I prefer, ... for his commandments are better and full of love

WHAT CAN A SORCERER (MAGICIAN) DO TO REPAIR HIS RELATIONSHIP WITH GOD?

Brother (sr) God is love, he does not seek to destroy the sorcerers (magicians) but he want to save their souls at the Last Judgement.

Brother (sr) you have to make the decision to abandon the devil power and accept the Lord Jesus Christ as your Lord, and Savior for he is the one God gave into the world so that all (no matter the age, sex , color, nationality, social status, etc ...) who will listen to his teachings, put into practice live forever. John 3:16

Brother (sr) you need to go through deliverance to be free of the devil. John 8:36

You, who are sorcerer or magician ,I know you have eyes that can see the true servants of God, use them and go to confess your sins to one of the servants to be free from the devil.
1 John 1:9, Acts 19:18-19

Brother (sr) do not be unbelieving, give your life to the Lord Jesus Christ because He is wonderful and very, very, very great.... and satan himself knows. 2 Chronicles 2:5 John 10:29, Marc5:6-13

Fear not, you will not die if you agree to confess your sins because the Lord Jesus Christ will protect you against death (against Satan). Psalms 97:10. John 17:12

May the God who put his words into my mouth to write to you be your power forever and ever.

" Sorcery (magic)
 Made Man
  to leave Eden "

In the beginning the earth was formless and empty, darkness was over the surface of the abyss, and the SPIRIT OF GOD was hovering over the waters as is the case at present.
The earth is again full of darkness as the days of the beginning, the devil is urging people to have his mark 666, the name of the beast as it is written in revelations13 :16-18 and further the devil invest with sorcery (magic, fetishism,...) children through cartoons.

Listen! The Lord Jesus said, you learned that it was said you do not commit adultery. But I tell you
That whoever looks at a woman lustfully
Has already committed adultery with her in his heart.
Matthew 5:27-28

Brother (sr)! Notice in the cartoons, you will find
Several practices of sorcery, magic, fetishism etc ..., and those practices give envy to children to have a supernatural power. In designing this idea the child is already becoming a prey of the devil.

When I say the world is again like the days of the beginning, you must understand that the spirit of God seeks where to live he is looking for men, women able to offer real light in the world, the Spirit of God seeks the one who can eat the flesh of the SON OF MAN and drink the blood of the SON OF MAN and who can teach men, women to do the same. Do not be surprised when reading this because it was by food that man was corrupt, likewise by food that man will be restored.
God created the earth cause he had the idea to form man, and if I can correct myself He had idea of creating a "god" like him.

Then God said, Let us make man in our image, after our likeness, and that he rules over the fish of the sea, over the livestock, over all the earth, and over every creeping thing that creeps on the earth. Genesis1: 26
In this passage, you will see that God has not only created man according to their image but also by their likeness.

Brother (sr) before continuing, I would like to answer your question:
Q / who was with God because you say according to their image, and their likeness?

-GOD was with his son Jesus Christ. Man is created by the image of God and Jesus, God and Jesus are one. JOHN 10:30

When God created the earth according to Genesis, the devil (satan) already existed but before being satan, he had the name of LUCIFER, he was a covering cherub, he put the seal of perfection, he was full of wisdom and perfect in beauty. He was in Eden, the garden of God, he was covered with all kinds of precious stones. Tambourines and flutes were in his service, prepared for the day he was created. God had placed him on the holy mountain of God, he was perfect in his ways until iniquity where found in him. EZEKIEL 28:11-15

Brother (sr) in this passage we see that God is the origin of Lucifer. God loved much Lucifer. He had given him a glory more than all the angels and because of the glory he had received from God, Lucifer revolted with some angels and God who is the source of power, has thrown him with all the angels who followed him. Ezekiel 28:16-19
revelations12:7-9, 12

After his fall, Satan who was Lucifer, now puts the seal to perdition, the mark of devil 666, the name of the beast to determine his children!
"The evil spirits, demons were already living on the earth, in the seas before God made man".

Brother (sr) If you look at the world's creation according to Genesis, is the second because in Ezekiel 28:13 God speaks in the mouth of his prophet that Lucifer was in Eden, the garden of God, he was covered with all kinds of stones precious carnelian, topaz, diamond, beryl, onyx, jasper, sapphire, of turquoise, emerald and of gold. Do not be surprised when I say the world according to Genesis is the second for this world also shall perish to have another world.

When God said, Let be light! Satan was already there.
Genese1: 3
-Let the earth bring forth grass, the
 yielding seed, and fruit trees yielding fruit after his kind,
Having them in their seed on the earth,

Satan already existed! Genese1: 11
-Let waters bring forth abundantly animals
 and let birds fly the earth across the expanse of the sky.
Satan existed! Genese1: 20

And when God said - let make man in our image, after
our Likeness, Satan still existed!
Genesis1: 26

I remember saying in the first letter of AKINI that the idea of The Tree of Knowledge of Good and Evil in the garden came from the devil and the devil is often in front of God for permission to tempt the children of GOD!

The world according to Genesis was done in the eyes of the devil and the devil was again jealous to see the garden that belonged to him was given to man. Man had become the guardian cherub of garden. With this desire (envy) that was the tree of knowledge of good and evil. Genesis 3: 4-5

KNOWLEDGE OF GOOD AND EVIL "

Listen! a sorcerer in any age (0-years .... years) knows how to judge! He knows the institutions of God which condemn man and institutions that justify man!
A sorcerer is inhabited by the spirit of the devil, satan, and because the devil has the Bible in him automatically
a witch also get this knowledge on good and
evil. MATTHIEU4 :1-11

Sorcerers (magicians) are judges for the devil, they use this knowledge of right and wrong to judge men in their sins! Himself the devil seduces men and after his seductions, he condemns man because the wages of sin is death.

God by his love prevented man from the tree of death and man complied with the instruction ,later one, God made a woman from the rib that he had taken from man. GENESIS 2: 23

Then the snake came to the woman!

The serpent (devil) is very crafty and cunning , he is seeking advantage over those who are not strong in faith in God. Revelation 12:9

HOW TO RESIST SATAN?

Do not like the world neither the things in the world.1 -The lust of the flesh, 2-lust of the eyes, and 3-the pride of life are the world. 1 John 2:14-17
you will see that these three responded into the woman after the speech of the devil.

* lust of the flesh- she saw the tree was good
to eat"

*lust of the eyes, she saw that the tree was accredited
 to view

*pride of life she saw that the tree was valuable
to open intelligence.

The cares of life gives access to the devil to destroy the souls of man.

DO NOT WE HAVE TO WORRY ABOUT LIFE?

If you read in the Book of Matthew 6:25-34 you will see that the Lord Jesus Christ was addressing a crowd about worries and concerns . Inverses 33-34 he says this: seek first the kingdom and justice of God and all these things will be over. Do not worry about tomorrow, for tomorrow will care for itself. Every day at a time.
Brother (sr) in MATTHEW 6: 33-34: The Lord Jesus makes us understand that God must be the first place into our life because if you put God in first place in your life and when you will be without job and your friend ask you to ally with an occult science for job you will refuse to serve mammon. MATTHEW 6:24

When the devil tempts you to sin and you do not give up your faith in God
For example:
- you,woman, you are suffering financially, and a married rich man offers you to be his concubine, and you refuse him because you know that God does not like adultery.

-You, man you are suffering financially and a rich woman and married

Propose you to be his boyfriend and refuse her because you know that God is against adultery.

- A rich man want to sleep with you, you man for money, you refuse him because you know that homosexuality is an abomination before God.

Leviticus 18:22 - you shall not sleep with a male as one sleep with a woman. That is an abomination

You who are homosexual, know that God loves you too, but He has not created man to have sex with another man, that's what he hates. Come back in sense! Run to God to deliver you from the seed of the devil by the power of the cross of his ONLY SON JESUS CHRIST.

- A rich woman wants you to be his wife, girlfriend, woman like her, you refuse her because you know it is an abomination before God.

God created woman to be woman to a man.
You who are lesbian know that God loves you too, but He does not created you to satisfy a woman like you, that's what he hates. Come back in sense! Run to God and the power of the cross of his son Jesus Christ will deliver you from the power of the devil (the devil's seed)

Leviticus 18:23 - you shall not sleep with a beast, for

Defiling yourself with it. The woman shall not approach
A beast to prostitute with it. It is a confusion. Lev20: 13-16

God condemns to death all those who have changed the use of sex! Leviticus 20: 13-16 and also gave the blood of the Lord Jesus Christ to bring to life those who make the decision to discontinue with misuse of sex.
When you do not sin then:
-God will raise and send a man to love you and you will not regret being married!

-God will raise and prosper you financially!

The passage from Matthew 6: 25-34 many Christians are using this to feed their weakness, and I do not want you to be their likeness!
Jesus Christ shows us that every things man believes that he can only get them by money, God is able to give without using money.

To confirm this, if you go back in Matthew 6:24 you will see that the Lord Jesus Christ spoke of God and money.

LEARN THAT YOU CAN:
- Dress without using money, you can eat without using money, you can be the owner of a house without buying it, you can be the owner of a shop without using money.
Do not be lazy, one that does not work does not eat either.

SO! DO NOT WE HAVE TO CARE FOR LIFE?

Everyone cares about life when he or she is a victim of poverty (rejection, suffering, illness,...). But do not let the cares and worries dominate you, because they will affect your faith and you can run to sin to get what you need.

"Life is more than food!

MY CHILD! Hear the word of your father:

"If you want to live, be ready to embrace death"
"Called death faithful friend and you will be spared from death"

My friend, through death that you will get your needs. That is why the Lord Jesus Christ said one day:

"Whoever wants to follow me, take up his cross and follow me"

When the devil comes to try a man, he makes sure to success in his mission! he closes all doors to bring him to obey him.

I would like to inform you that there are three temptations of the devil to man:
-1.On materials
-2.On the flesh
-3. On the soul

To talk about three temptations of the devil, I would like to use these passages from the Bible:

-Job 1:6-12
-Job 2:1-7
-Matthew 4:1-11

TEMPTATION ON MATERIALS

-Job 1:6-12 - or the son of God came one day
Before the LORD, and Satan came also among
 them. And the Lord said to Satan: Where are you from?
And Satan answered the LORD to walk the earth
And to walk around. The Lord said to Satan: did you
Considered my servant Job? There is person
Like him on earth: he is a man fully integrate
And upright, fearing God and turning away from evil.
And Satan answered the LORD, is this a way of
Disinterested Job fear God? Do you not
Protected him, his house, and everything to him?
You have blessed the work of his hands, his cattle
and his land. But put forth your hand now, and touch
All that belongs to him and I am sure that he
will curse you in front.

The Lord said to Satan:

This is all that belongs to him, do
Not put hands on his soul.
Brother (sr), Satan can never love to see you in peace, abundance, assured for salvation for he has no more room in THE BOOK OF LIFE. He also wants to see you abscent into the book, that is way he tempts man.
Job was blameless and upright, although very rich, he feared God and eschewed evil because of his integrity. God had held a council with his sons about Job, and Satan came also among them!

When you please God a lot, God will also hold a council for you, to glorify you. That is why the Lord Jesus Christ said:

"-He who loves a lot, he will be forgiven a lot" (in other terms: he will be much graced)

WHO ARE THE SONS OF GOD?

To not shock you, I would like to mention two: MOSES AND ELIJAH. If God calls us sons of God (Christians)

Therefore there is nothing surprising to call MOSES and ELIJAH sons of God, they even spoke to the Lord Jesus-Christ before his death on the cross. Matthew 17:3

Satan knows that man is too materialistic that is why he asked permission from God to touch the goods of job, and he was sure of misery in which he will put job, job will curse God, but to his surprise the kingdom and the righteousness of God was first in the life of Job. Job 1: 13-22

"You have to wait for the Intervention of the devil in your life - in your home, -in your work place – in your business. -in your studies and never be happy if you are not been yet through temptation, that I can call test for God".

 Joy comes after the tears as the Lord Jesus Christ said: -

Blessed are they which are persecuted for righteousness, for the Kingdom of Heaven is theirs. Matthew 5:10

Fortunate are those who mourn, for they shall be comforted. Matthew 5: 4

.TEMPTATIONS OF THE FLESH

In this part, I would like also to talk about myself!

In the month of February 2002, a year after my consecration pastoral the man of God PASTEUR RICHARD N 'KONJI OF " CHRISTIAN ASSEMBLY THE THRONE OF GRACE" ACTG (4. 02. 2001)

(- Pastor Richard N' Konji was a great inspiration for me to accept the Lord Jesus Christ for My eternal master. When I returned from presidential college of GBADO, I resolved myself to live in a pagan - July 1995, I mean begin to do everything that a young man can do in his youth ". I had some plot of programs with some friends on how to rule.
Back in Kinshasa (DR Congo) - July 1995 my mother-YOMBO YAKAMBILI-MARIE-JOSE, leaded me to the church where she prayed. " My father-NDONINGBA SAMBIA-LOUISON was abscent.
Arriving at the church, Pastor Richard N 'KonjI was preaching about The Lord's meal and I can assure you that in listening to the teaching, I was very frightened and I made the decision in me to not eat even if one gives me!

And at the end of worship, he announced a retreat program in Kinsuka.
The day of the retreat my mom asked me to go with her and I refused and told my mother: my uncle stays also in Kinsuka , I, I will go to uncle, and you will go to fast and we found a conclusion!

Reached Kinsuka, Mom took me to a different route than that of my uncle, and then, I display the anger and mum begged me, saying where we are going, there is a house, you, you will be in the house and we, we will be out! After his speech I acted as a good boy.

Arrived at the place of retreat, there was no way to be alone, while others were outside. And I said to myself: "I will not consider their speech." When Pastor Richard N 'Konji has finished speaking, he asked everyone to go rest and come back after for confession.
When we were leaving, he stopped to tell us that the Lord has said:-a person did not took into consideration his word and l have acknowledged that it was me.

He restarted to preach. My brother, my sister when I put serious to listen, I did not stop to be amazed at the inside of me the way that he preached the gospel of Christ - with full knowledge, wisdom, intelligence , and I say to me - so if I accept the Lord Jesus Christ, i will be good as him? - I will also speak with full of knowledge? .... Based on these questions within me, I agreed to deceive the Lord Jesus Christ for the Leader of my life. I decided to follow the Lord Jesus with all my heart, my whole soul and with all my strength to become "WISE "

I am no longer following the Lord Jesus Christ for wisdom but rather because "HE HAS THE WORD OF LIFE" and He is the tree of life ". I understood that wisdom comes by the fear of GOD! Pastor Richard N Konji was and remains for me the most important man on earth and no one can take his place for through him, I know the Lord Jesus Christ in truth .- May God bless my mom also for her work)

Every time I think of my father Richard, I cry bitterly. May GOD does not stop me to cry my father every time my heart is saddened.

My father Richard N 'Konji did not give me the chance to choose between good and evil.

I was always asked to choose good! What I am, is his work.

Papa Richard N'Konji :
-Thanks for preaching me the Lord Jesus Christ!
-Thanks for accepting to be my
spiritual father!
-Thank for you taught me to choose
only good!

DADDY, you remain engraved in my heart forever! I love you.

My great sadness is that he is dead and buried in my absence while I was also tortured by disease, he will never know my wife, my children, he will never see the work of God in my hands. When I left Kinshasa, I thought that we will meet again, he will preach in the Ministry God has given me.

"- May God bless the biological children of my father! – May God be your father - May the light of the Most High shine on your paths - whoever who will raise to war you fails – May your tears sadden the heart of God .-Be pleased to have N'Konji for father.

I got sick. I had a cough that did not end. I went to see clinical doctors to determine the disease in question, but they could not, even tuberculosis was not found in me after the culture of sputum, and cough was not ending. The Cough i had,I define it as the definition of a cough.

At July 2002 while I was sleeping, I have had a vision and in this vision, my spirit was transported, and I found myself in a long, wide avenue and suddenly one thing in the form of a human being appeared before me and smelling very badly and a voice calls me and says, "AKINI! He who stands before you is a demon ", and when the voice stop talking, the demon addresses me:" AKINI! because of the word of god that is in your mouth. WE WILL ELIMINATE YOU PHYSICALLY "- HE WAS VERY SERIOUS ABOUT HIS MESSAGE! After he disappeared, then I woke up. I was like a dead on the bed for an hour. On hour was like a few seconds!....There was a clock on the wall.
And when I rose up, I have awakened my brother in the Lord, the Evangelist Samuel Phoba (- who was in charge of the first publication of the letter of Akini - on 28.mai.2011) I told him all about and then I laughed because I know who lives in me he is stronger than Satan and his demons.

One night after 40 days, I was in my bedroom and I felt like one hit something on my chest and I run fast to the window to take out what was in my mouth and i was vomiting blood and the blood was mixed with round things (I do not know how to explain it but not only in liquid)
And soon I called my mom (YOMBO-MARIE JOSE, could not give birth to a boy and this became a problem in her marriage. And she had made a vow to God:

: - If you give me a boy, I will give him to you. One day during her sleep, she had a dream - she was standing with one of her sisters and a little boy approaching them, and behind them was a very pretty woman with long hair who sang with an angelic voice and told the boy to choose one of those women!
The boy chose YOMBO YAKAMBILI and later one mom was pregnant and bore a son in the name of DIEUDONNE (DEDE): THE GIFT OF GOD).

I was vomiting in a pot, my mom was throwing the blood.

My brother (sr) the pains I felt in my body, you can not have them and continue to live if God is not with you. I felt my bones shake and my spine shaked when I coughed, the hemoptysis (vomiting blood) was not stopping.

Every day after these 40 days, I was vomiting blood. More than two months I was not sleeping on the bed because when I was trying to lengthen , at the same time I was vomiting blood in quantity and for that, I was forced to sit on a chair, my head against the bed , and by that position my feet becoming big. I was again receiving injections to pee a lot. On that position my back was bent and I was unable to sit up straight. II did not also want to exercise to straighten me because I felt relieved at least in that position.

"I was unable to lift a fork or a glass of water to put in my mouth, because when I forced myself, I was vomiting blood in quantity." When I was seeing my child, my Nephew Gabriel (6 years) carrying a can of 5 liters of water, I wondered in my heart if one day I can also do it.

I bless the LORD GOD for swiping my tears night and day. I can carry a can of 50 liters without vomiting blood or even coughing!

I want to say one thing and God is my witness.
"When my pain was increasing, I was
closing my eyes and I said, LORD JESUS CHRIST! I want to say one thing and I know you read the Heart of Man and you know what I want to tell you comes from my Heart:

"Lord Jesus Christ, I love you whatever my pain and I know that your love for me is more than my love for you, you are every things to me. The gift of eternal life that you have given me is the best thing for me, I will always worship you forever.
One day, a doctor at academic hospital in Kinshasa told me this after explaining what I felt in my body "- AKINI! These are just your thoughts "
And I realized that he was not wrong to say it because it was incredible effects. -Image you arein the torture of the devil.

Two years later, arrived in South Africa my body did not responded positively, and I remember, more than twice having to beg God to allow me to die.
And one day, I have done the will to anger God to let death take me away because I did not want again to live but I did not ceased my prayer of worship:

"I love you Lord Jesus Christ whatever my pains and I know that your love for me is more than my love for you, you are everything to me, the gift of eternal life that you have given me is the best thing for me, I will always worship you !
My brother, the name of the Jesus Christ has the power to strengthen the legs and confuse the minds of men.
Your disease is for the glory of GOD! God wants to show himself by !

One day! "I was alone in the room that we shared with three people, and around 4 p.m , I have started to vomit blood and I did not want to warn neighbors door. Around 5 p.m as vomiting did not stopped, I saw that this was no longer good to keep silence. And those who were there found a private car to take me to the hospital (Kalafong hospital- pretoria west). I was deposited at the gate of the fence, I asked them to let me inside but they would no. There alone, I continued to vomit blood. I could not walk, I was lying down on the floor infront of the fence;
I called the keeper who was in front of me to tell him to inform inside that there is a sick outside.

And the gentleman looked at me and say if you do not walk yourself to go inside, you will die here. "He refused.
- May God forgive him. And I closed my eyes and tell my JESUS:
   "Lord give me the strength to walk", I got up and walked quickly to the inside and by far a nurse saw me and came to help, carried me with the wheelchair.
I continued to vomit blood, all those who saw me were saying: it is over for me, I was going to die, and a mother looked at me and say "my child believe in God and you will not die"-May GOD bless the fruit of her womb! - Because I felt affection by her.
after 8 p.m i stopped vomitying blood and I was admitted to the hospital.
You who listen to me, your love is very important for those who are sick at your side. Affection brings joy to the heart and that joy can improve the condition of the patient.
"I was deprived of affection during my tears in South Africa when" I was tormented by disease and I had developed a serious headache.

When I dared to worry, in less than a minute, I had a strong headache. I felt like my head was divided, and I was forced to control not to worry because worries were killing me again!

But God was and is with me, He brings joy to my heart, he was saying to my heart that he loves me and he is preparing me to bear his name ".
Every time I think about my pains, I praise God (I'm serious and God is my witness) for allowing the devil to touch my body!

"It is by fire that you will bear a name before the LORD"
- You who haven not yet experienced the baptism of fire, do not be happy because by the fire gold shines!

I live and will live throughout the years as my father Jesus Christ will desire!

Never feared the devil satan. He is a bully!

This temptation has done what I am today! trough pains, crying, sufferings GOD made me MAN!

One of my lungs was destroyed, and when I have been informed and I have to go through surgery, my heart and I, had cried a lot, but God answered me in this passage from the Bible
2corientiens 12: 1 - 10 and I realized that God wanted that one of my lungs to be destroyed for me to be HIS HAND. "- The blade did not touch my body after my transfer in South Africa ".

The GOD who appeared to me into FIRE and spoke to me mouth to mouth - December 1999 swipes my tears days and nights.

In December 1999, I was seriously ill, I had TB!
One night while I slept, my spirit was transported to a mountain, and on top of the mountain ,was a Fire and when I wanted to go up to the fire, a voice came from the fire to tell me to take off my sandals for the place where I stand is holy!
And after I took off, I approached the fire, and a voice came out of the fire again and say, "AKINI! AKINI! What do you want me to do for you?

After answering HIM HE disappeared .I woke up!

The next day, while I slept, I have received a vision:
This is the vision: - I have seen an old man and gave me the mission to go to free blacks in slavery of
White!

Listen to the explanation:

- Blacks are the ones who are under the power of the devil, those who have Mark of perdition 666, the name of the beast:-witches, magicians, witch doctors, Those who practice the forbidden etc.
....

- Blacks included: the Europeans-Americans, Asians, Africans and Oceans

- Whites are Satan, his demons and evil spirits.

When I went on a mission, I found a barrier, and there were giants soldiers who cut (incisions)people and put a powder into injuries to invest them with the power of the devil.

They asked me to lie down on my back and they started to put the cuts on me, when they were cutting my body, I was praying to God and invoking the blood of the Lord Jesus Christ to destroy their work on me.

After the incisions, they started putting the powder and while they put, I felt nothing in me for the blood of the Lord Jesus Christ has destroyed the power of powder, but they were sure that the powder did its job and when I got up, I have used wisdom to show them I was actually invested.

After that, I went on a vast territory and there were large prisons buildings with full of prisoners.

There were plenty of soldiers that were circulating well-armed. I circulated in the territory and I traveled throughout the territory to see the prisons and prisoners.

Their leader knew that I was on a mission and he proposed me to make me rich if I accept to abandon the mission!

I rejected the offer and surprisely he could not stop me, I, alone in his territory.

I walked in peace without fear among his soldiers on his territory!

I have contacted all the prisoners and I told them that we will fight for freedom and all were in agreement with me and told them on my signal, we will attack those whites.

At my signal all the prisons were broken and there was a very large number of blacks who came out of prisons, and where the territory was limited, there was an ocean,
And in the ocean canoes emerged from the bottom of the ocean filled with blacks inside in a point the entire ocean was filled with canoes, and together we attacked those whites and we killed them all.
 I have seized their leader and went on top of a tall building, at the height of between earth and clouds, and I threw him down.

I spoke on myself to encourage you to stand firm in faith in the Lord Jesus Christ despite your suffering!

You, who are sick a long time, never believe that God has abandoned you. He will turn your tears into joy, you will sing a new song: "I was sick and the Lord JESUS healed me, alleluia ..! Hosanna to the SON OF GOD"

"Do not fear the devil when he threatens you by witches, magicians for all is accomplished on the cross." Satan has been brought to nothing.

LISTEN MY CHILD! :

- The earth is the footstool of God and
Satan is the master of the land for a
Time, and it concluded that God walks
Over Satan. MATTHEW 5: 35
Revelation 12: 12

If we go back to the story of Job, we will see that after the first failure, the devil returned to the LORD for permission to touch his flesh. Job 2: 1-7

The devil knows that when a man is seriously ill, it is easy to loose faith and accepts anything for his recovery but despite all, Job did not sin with his lips. Job 2: 10
Be careful with your lips when you go through difficult times, because by your lips, you can bury yourself, and also you can build your place with God.

3. TEMPTATION ON THE SOUL

Matthew 4:1-11 after Jesus Christ was baptized, the spirit took him into the wilderness to be tempted by
The devil. Matthew 4:1

- The first temptation of Jesus was on food (materials)

Matthew 4: 2-4 - after fasting forty days and Nights he was hungry.
The tempter being approached, he said, if you
Are the son of God, command that these stones
Made bread.
JESUS said, it is written: Man does
Not live by bread alone but by every
Word that proceeds from the mouth of God.

• The second temptation was in the flesh.
Matthew 4: 5-7 - the devil took him in the city
Holy placed him on top of the temple
And said if you are son of God, cast
Thyself down: for it is written about you
He will give his angels orders
On your subject, and they shall bear thee
Hands, lest your foot
Strikes against stone.

• THE THIRD TEMPTATION WAS ON THE SOUL

Matthew 4: 8-11, the devil took him up again on a
Very high mountain, showed him all the
Kingdoms of the world and their glory, and he
Said, I will give you all these things if you
 fall down and worship me.

The devil was trying to win the soul of the Lord Jesus!
The Lord Jesus said to him, Get away Satan! For it is written:
Thou shall worship the Lord your God and you will
serve him alone. Then the devil left. And here
Angels came to Jesus and they serve him.

The purpose of Satan in all his persecution is to bring you to worship him. However, by associating to an occult science (rose cross, maicari, framasson, incacare, etc.) you pronounce yourself the devil's disciple.

I have already said, the Lord Jesus walk on Satan! This means: The Lord Jesus walk on the suffering. The Lord Jesus walk on the famine. The Lord Jesus walk on poverty. The Lord Jesus walk on unemployment. The Lord Jesus walk on celibacy. The Lord Jesus walk on infertility. The Lord Jesus walk on disease. The Lord Jesus walk on aids. The Lord JESUS walk on diabetes. The Lord Jesus walk on Cancer. The Lord Jesus walk on TB. The Lord Jesus walk on infirmity. The Lord Jesus walk on traps. The Lord Jesus walk on death. The Lord Jesus walk on blindness. The Lord Jesus walk on nakedness. The Lord Jesus walking on anything that can hurt you! ...

Never fear the devil satan, he is a big loser!

The devil has also sought to lead me to worship him! When I landed at the airport of Oliver Tambo (RSA) a white man had a great interest to me, just like that! As I wanted to leave him, he gave me his card of address, and I have saw the sign of a certain sect, and refused.

Within a week, a Gabonese get interested to me while I was making a call in a public phone;

He told me that he knows a way in which I can earn $ 1,000 - $ 10,000 every day without providing any effort. He left me all his contacts in my notebook. And because I had with me the contacts of the man, the devil had taken the opportunity to talk to me in the ear for at least two months to accept the case!
And one day, I have realized that I was making a big mistake to keep these contacts and I had erased them from my book to free myself from the trap.

Note: The devil is very cunning, he uses trickery to attract and invest men his power by force.

When I say the devil is a loser, I'm not kidding!
One night while I was still sick in Kinshasa - 2003, one of my paternal uncles told the entire family that I was dead!
And at the same night a group of people came to mourn me, but they did not entered in the plot because they had not heard the sound of weeping and returned.
In the morning we began to receive people for my mourning, and when they came, my mother knocked on my door, I came out, I greeted them and laughed. For one week we received people for my mourning.

Actually that night, I was dead. I, who speak to you, I am a living witness that "the Lord Jesus Christ is the resurrection and life"

"You know! That night, I slept and when I opened my
Eyes, I saw that I was lying straight up as a
Dead in the coffin, and I was much worried all night.
In the morning when I heard the news which was spread that night, I understood directly that the devil had killed my body as he had sworn, but the Lord Jesus Christ raised me while he was busy celebrating.

Returning to the conversation of the serpent, you will find that the devil offered a power to woman. And the woman after eating from the tree of knowledge of good and evil, and gave also unto her husband, the eyes of one and the other opened.

The eyes of the one and the other opened in the words of the serpent!

Witchcraft is transmitted by something eatable: - sweet - biscuit-cake-a banana-mango-risk meat - fish etc ...

Magic also is transmitted after being at the table of demons!
A sorcerer, magician has eyes that see the invisible what the normal eyes can not see. That's why you will find that the Magi arrived in Jerusalem from orient and seek the King of the Jews Jesus Christ who was born because they have seen his star and came to worship him. Matthew 2 1-20

"Mages are astrologers (those who study the stars) and they are in abomination before God. Deuteronomy 18: 9-14
Deuteronomy 18: 9-14 - when you come into the country
That the Lord thy God given thee, thou shall
Not learn to imitate the abomination of those nations that not be found among you and no one that put
his son or daughter in the fire.

No one who works as a diviner of astrologer, of augurs, and magicians, who consults with those who call The spirits or dissent adventure, person interviewed the dead. Anyone who does these things is detestable to the eternal, and because of these abominations that the Lord your God will cast out these nations before you. You shall be blameless unto the LORD thy God. For these nations you will dispossess listened to soothsayers and diviners but you, the Lord your God, do not allow it.

One thing that surprise me, the astrologers are in abominations to the Lord, but they went to worship the Lord Jesus, more, God himself led them to where the young child was.

WHAT DOES IT MEAN?

My brother (sr) it is done to justify that every knee will bow before the name of the Lord Jesus Christ.

And to give us the assurance about the Lord Jesus that He is actually the son of GOD! However, even Satan himself acknowledges that the Lord Jesus is truly God's son, then why do you doubt? - Remember that God dialogue with Satan, his demons and those inhabited unclean spirits (witches, magicians, witchdoctors etc. ..) Numbers 22: 1-30

WHY DOES CHRISTMAS EXIST?

Nowhere the Lord Jesus nor his disciples celebrated the Christmas! The world celebrates Christmas without understanding what really is happening - the 25 / 12 of each year.
Listen! On Christmas Day Satan and his demons bow down and worship the Jesus Christ not because they love him but rather to show that they are scared of him .- It is a very special day for them! Psalms 97:7

Psalms 97:7
 - They are confused, all those who serve
Images, who glory idols.
All gods bow down before him.
* Witches, magicians, witch doctors, anyone who practices the forbidden, your gods bow down before the Lord Jesus Christ"

SO DO WE NOT HAVE TO CELEBRATE CHRISTMAS?

I do not think that is a sin when you celebrate the birth of the Lord Jesus, but only the biggest party you should celebrate is the death of the Lord Jesus because we are saved and forgiven of sins by it. Luke 22:14-20 it
Listen Another testimony about the Lord Jesus Christ and this time by demons

Matthew 5:1-13: - they reached the other side of the sea, in the country of the Gadarenes. as soon as Jesus was out of the boat, he came to meet him
A man out of the tombs and possessed of an unclean spirit. This man had his home in sepulcher and no one could bind him, even with chains, but he had broken chains and broken the fetters and nobody had the strength of dompt him. he was constantly night and day among the tombs and the mountains shouting, and cutting himself with stones saw Jesus from afar, he ran and bow down before him and cried with a loud voice what wrong between me and you, "Jesus, son of the Most High God" I beg to you in the name of God do not torment me.

For Jesus said to him: "Come out of him
Unclean spirit." And asking: what is
Your name? My name is Legion, he replied
him, for we are many. And he prayed instantly
 not send them out of the country.
There was a swine feeding. And
Devils besought him, saying, send us
In these swine, that we enter into them. He gave them leave. And
unclean spirits came out
In the herd rushing slopes
Steep into the sea: there were about
Two thousand, and they were drowned in the sea

WHY DID THE LORD JESUS DRIVE UNCLEAN SPIRITS IN THE HERD OF SWINE?

Listen! The Lord Jesus Christ is the definition of love!
Unclean spirits know that their sites are in unclean places! A pig is considered unclean before God and the Lord Jesus knew their places are in unclean places, that is why he allowed them to enter into the swine.

I know the apostle Paul spoke sanctifying unclean food!
However if you can and then the pagan?

Several diseases are caused by unclean food that God has forbidden man to eat!

- Even you, a prophet, you know when God shows you a pig in a vision, you know already that he speaks of impurity!

I know that Apostle Paul spoke of food and asks us not to judge on that!

However if your conscience does not reproach you, eat with thanksgiving!

I do not believe that the door to hell (the lake of fire) can be opened for those who ate a pork, shrimp, etc. ... but what is certain, the door opens for fornicators, idolaters, liars, thieves, etc....

He who does not eat the unclean food, does a great thing because it is spared of disease!

He who eats them expose himself to diseases! He who eats, let him not eat frequently for his health! Protect yourself and God will protect you.

"Beloved! Let me talk a little bit about land of Promise, the country of Israel!

I asked myself many questions, why does GOD gave to his people (the seed of Abraham) a country that belonged to other people? Could not he give them another territory? Instead of chasing others!

To answer your question, I would like us to read in Genesis 9: 18-27

Genesis 9: 18-27 - the son of Noah who came out of the ark were Shem, Ham and Japheth. ham was the
Father of Canaan. These are the three, the son of
Noah and that is all that populated the earth. Noah began to cultivate the land planted vines. He drank wine, he drunk and was uncovered within his tent. ham
Father of Canaan, saw the nakedness of his father
And he brought out to these brothers. Then
Shem and Japheth took a garment, they put
on their shoulders, and went covered the nakedness of their father.
As their faces were turned away, they did
Not see the nakedness of their father.

When Noah awoke from his wine, and knew
What had made him his youngest son. And he said:
Cursed be Canaan; let him being the slave of
slave of his brothers! He said again, blessed be
the Lord God of Shem, and Canaan shall be
Their slave! God shall enlarge the possession of Japheth, that he
lived in tents of Shem, and Canaan shall be his slave!

Brother (sr) ham is the father of the nations that God had cast out. And Abraham is the seed that Noah had blessed, Shem!

Thereby understand that there was already curse on ham, ham was called to be slave of Shem and GOD did fulfill the word of his servant NOAH.

"The good news is that time has come where by God is no more worshiped in Jerusalem neither on mountain but in spirit and in truth. John 4:20-24

The Holy Land is a place where men and women worship the God of Abraham, Isaac, and Jacob in spirit and in truth.
IS IT A SIN TO DRINK ALCOHOL?

Just above we have the story of a righteous man Noah who was devalued to one of his son ham because of the alcohol.
Alcohol is not good, he takes out man's proud and leads to destruction!
Many pregnancies are under the influence of alcohol and even AIDS. Under alcohol man becomes uncontrollable. Alcohol makes one blind and a blind man does not know the path.

To get rid of the blindness so say no to alcohol! And seek God through the Lord Jesus to set you free from alcohol!
I know that many calling themselves Christians, and pagans are using the wedding feast where the Lord Jesus changed water into wine. John 2: 1-12 to defend their drunkenness!

God does not force anyone to obey him! He always put before man life and good, death and
Life .Déuteronome30: 15

God is not a dictator, he leaves man to make his choice

To do better the work of God, you have to abstain from alcohol, that is why God forbade all Nazirean alcohol. Judges 13: 4-5

LISTEN to: Luke 1: 15
- Because he will be great before the LORD. he
Shall drink neither wine nor strong drink, and
Will be filled with the HOLY SPIRIT from the womb
Of his mother. (The angel is talking to Zechariah father of JOHN-BAPTIST)

THE HOLY SPIRIT DOES NOT WORK WITH ALCOHOL!

'The good news is that the lord Jesus christ has made us priests (christians) with his blood so that we may be filled with the holy spirit to do his work. Revelation 5: 9-10

If you believe that the Lord Jesus Christ made you priest by his blood to do the work of God, then answer this question: ***"IS IT GOOD FOR A PRIEST TO DRINK ALCOHOL?***

These people were already drunk and Jesus has done it under pressure! Pressure brings God to give man his need (good or bad)

TO CONCLUDE:
- The one who wants to drink alcohol to feed his drunkenness let him continuing because the Lord Jesus changed water into wine!
- The one who believes that alcohol leads to evil, let him be happy because he sees now!

GENESIS 3: 22:
- God recognized that man was having another
Power in him (the evil power) because
He said: Here the man is become as one of
Us to the knowledge of good and evil.
And now, let's prevent him to the tree of life to
Eat and live forever. Here we see clearly that man was separated from GOD because he had another power
In him, that I call the power of the devil!

WAS GOD JEALOUS OF MAN?

You have to be crazy to say that God was jealous of man. God drove out man because he chose to listen and to obey the devil Satan!

When you accept satan for father, God excludes you from the tree of life!

"Is not true that you can not inherit from a person you rejected? "When man ate of the tree had become like a god," him who was like God"

NOTE: DO NOT MISS THE SPEECH OF AKINI!

> **"WE ARE LIKE**
> **GOD FOR**
> **KNOWLEDGE OF LIFE"**

When man ate of the tree had become like a god, the spirit of the devil entered into him!
A sorcerer, a magician, etc ... works like a god!
Several witches, magicians, etc. ..are in distress but they are afraid to break away from the devil satan because their afraid of death! And it is our duty as Christian to ensure them salvation, life in the Lord Jesus Christ.
Listen,Sorcerer, magician ! Partake in the blood and
Flesh of Christ which he partaked himself
That through death (his death) he might destroy him
Who has the power of death, i mean the devil
Satan and to deliver them who through fear
Of death were all their lifetime subject to
Servitude. Heubrew2: 13-15

Now, what are you waiting for? Arise, be baptized, and wash away your sins in the name of the Lord JESUS CRHIST

Listen! You have become sorcerer after eating human flesh and drank his blood to a form of food, for that you also need to eat the flesh and drink the blood of the Lord Jesus Christ so that the Spirit of God may dwell in you.
"The one God protects , the devil (Satan) can not touch and you know as well".

"The name of the Lord Jesus Christ is over Satan and you know it too because every time, Christians speak of the Lord Jesus Christ you are in trouble in your missions. You also know when Satan and his demons hold captive a person and a servant of God cast out demons from a person in the name of the Lord Jesus Christ, they obey and leave the person. However, as you know it all, use it therefore to abandon the devil satan forever.

"Listen good news! The Lord Jesus Christ was also crucified for witches, magicians, witchdoctors, diviners, astrologers, those who call on spirits or dissent fortunes, who interrogates the dead, those who do spend their son or daughter in the fire etc ...

This means that God has opened the door of life to those who serve Satan, to lay their hands to the tree of life to eat and live forever. HEUBREW 8: 12

Revelation 13: 16-18: - and she did all, both small and great, rich and poor, free and slaves, to receive a mark on their right hand or on their foreheads
And that no man might buy or
Sale, without the brand name of
The beast or the number of his name.
Here is wisdom. He who has
The understanding count the number
Of the beast. For it is a number
Of man, and his number is six hundred
Sixty-six (666)

Brother (sister)! We are already living the fulfillment of
Revelations13: 16-18 which the devil imposes
Inhabitants of the earth to receive the mark of
666 for progress, success, celebrity etc ...
Indeed, anyone who becomes a member
Of an occult science (Rosicrucians, maicari, incacare,
Framasson etc ...) get this mark.
- *"THE MARK IS INVISIBLE FOR MANY!"*

The world is like the days of Noah whereby the people walked according to the course of the world!

You know that currently all over the world men and women integrate in occult science (Rosicrucians, maicari, framasson, etc ...) to be employed to find promotion,- to maintain their positions, -to dominate, -to customers -to get rich -to be famous, -to attract attention of people -to win in competitions, -to protect themselves against murder, -to go from classes- to win in elections, -to have the authority etc. ...

And by becoming a disciple, the devil, Satan opens the door to his disciple because he accepted the mark of destruction, the name of the beast by worshiping him.

WHAT IS THE FATE OF THOSE WHO HAVE NOT THE MARK OF PERDITION 666?

Blessed are those who have not the mark of destruction 666, the name of the beast for they will see the face of GOD! And they will have the mark of perfection 'the name of the son of God Jesus and God will gives us power to overcome Satan and all his kingdom forever and ever:

"LET HOLY PEOPLE SAYS: AMEN! and one who wants to wash himself to the blood of the lord Jesus christ says: amen! "

Blessed are those who have the mark of perfection "because they will never see evil. We will judge Satan and his kingdom.

THE BOOK OF HIS TRIAL IS ALREADY OPENED BY THE LAMB OF GOD TO THROW HIM INTO THE LAKE OF FIRE AND SULPHUR. Revelation 5: 1-14

"*He who believes that the mark of perfection, the name of the son of God Jesus christ is the best, do this*:
-Close your eyes, feel the presence of the Lord Jesus Christ before you and say 7 times:

-Lord Jesus Christ, *you are life!*
-Lord Jesus christ, you are life!
-Lord Jesus christ, you are life!
-Lord Jesus christ, you are life!
-Lord Jesus christ, you are life!
-Lord Jesus christ, you are life!
-Lord Jesus christ, you are life!

Brother, sister to inherit the kingdom of heaven, you must be willing to go through the pain because it is the way to glory! *- is better at the end of a thing than its starting!*

The Lord Jesus Christ warned us well before so that we do not curse GOD during the Tribulation to come,CHRISTIANS!

Let us be ready to die for Christ, ready to cry for Christ, ready to be hated for Christ! ...

Let us arm ourselves **with faith apostles had in the lord Jesus christ against anti-christ.**

Listen! Acts 4: 13-20:
- when they saw the assurance of
Peter and John, they were astonished
Knowing that they were men
Without instructions, and they recognized
them had been with Jesus.
But as they saw near
Them the man who was healed, they
Had nothing to say. They
Ordered everybody out of the Sanhedrin, and they deliberate among themselves, saying: what shall we do with these men?

For it is clear to all
Inhabitants of Jerusalem that a miracle reported was done by them
And we can not deny it.
But to stop thing spreading
Advantage among the people
Defend them with threatens
Now to not talk to anyone either
That name. They called them, and
defend them to speak and
To teach in the name of Jesus.
Peter and John answered them
Judge for *yourself, we have to obey to*
God, rather than you because we can not
talk about what we have seen and heard.

Listen! Acts 5: 17-28:
- But the high-priest
 and all those with
Him, namely of sadducceens
Rose, filled with envy, put hands on the apostles, and
Threw them in the public prison.
But an angel of the Lord, having
Open during the night the doors of
The prison, brought them out, and say:
go, stay in the temple
and teach to the people all
the words of this life. Having
Heard this, they came from the
Morning in the temple, and began
To teach.

The high priest and those
Who were with him took place,
and they called all the sanhedrin
The elders of the son of Israel, and
Sent to bring the apostles from the
Prison. The ushers, they went and not
Found them in the prison.
They returned and made their
Report, saying we have find
 the prison securely locked,
And the guards who were before the
Doors, but after opening,
We did not found anyone
. When they heard
These words, the commander of the tem-
Ple and the chief priests
Did not know what to think of the apostles

And suddenly Someone
 came to tell them: Here, men
You have put in prison are
In the temple and teaching the
People. Then the captain went
With the officers, and led
Without violence, because they were afraid
Of being stoned by the people. After
That they had brought them in the presence
Of The Sanhedrin, the high-priest
 asked them in these terms
"we do not defend you
the teaching in the name of Jesus? and here, you have filled
jerusalem with your
teaching, and you want to make us

responsible of the blood of this man!
Listen! Acts 5: 29-32:

- Peter and the apostles answered
We must obey God rather than to
Men. The God of our fathers
Raised Jesus, whom you killed in
A tree. God has him in
his right hand as Prince and savior
to give Israel the
REPENTANCE AND FORGIVENESS OF
SINS. We are witness of those things, as well as the Holy Ghost,
whom God has given to those who
Obey him.

Listen! Acts 6: 7-15:
- The word of God spread
Increasing the number of disciples
Multiplied greatly in Jerusalem

And a large number of priests
Obeyed to the faith.
Stephen, full of grace and power, did wonders and
Great miracles among the people.
Some members of the synagogue
Known as freedmen, from that of
Cyreniens and that of the Alexandrian
With Jews of Cilicia and Asia,
Began to question him, but they could not
 resist the wisdom and
spirit in which he spoke. Then
They suborned men
Said, "we have heard saying blasphemous words
Against Moses and against God

They stirred up the people, the old
And scribbles, and throwing themself on him,
They seized him, and they took him to
Sanhedrin. They produced false
Witnesses, who said this man
Cease not to utter words against
The holy place and against the law because we
have heard saying of Jesus that,
Nazarite will destroy this place, and change
Our customs which Moses delivered us.
 All those who sat in Sanhedrin having set eyes on
Stephen, his face seemed to them like that of an angel.

Listen! Acts 7: 51-60:

- stiff-necked people, uncircumcised
of Heart and Earrings!. You
Always resist the Holy Spirit

What were your fathers, you are
Too. which of your prophets your father did not persecute? They
killed those who announced in advance
The coming of the fair, you have killed now, and you
Have been murderers you who have received
The law by the commandments
OF ANGELS, and that you did not
Keep them! On hearing these words ...
They were furious in their hearts
And they ground their teeth against him.
But he, being full of Holy Esprit, and fixing the eyes to the Sky,
saw the glory of God and Jesus
Standing at the right hand of God

They then drove loudly
And stopped their ears, and they
Rushed together upon him
Dragged him out of the city, and the
Stoned him. The witnesses laid down
Their garments at the feet of a
 man named Saul (THE APOSTLE
PAUL) and they stoned Stephen,
He prayed and said: Lord Jesus,
Receive my spirit! STEPHEN BEING
Knelt, he cried in an
Loud voice, Lord, Do
Not impute this sin. AND HE SLEPT.

Listen! Acts 12: 1 -11:

- About the same time, the King He-
Rode began to mistreat some
Members of the church,

And he did kill by the sword JACQUES
Brother of John. Seeing that this was
Pleasing to the Jews, he arrested
Peter this was during the days of
Unleavened bread. After entering
And thrown into prison, he put him in the gar-
Of four squads of four
Soldiers each, with the intention of
To appear before the people
 after pass over .PIERRE
Kept in prison. And the church did not
Cease to address prayers for him
Forward GOD. The night that preceded the
Day when Herod was going to do comparative, PETER, bound with two chains
Sleeping between two soldiers

And sentries at the door
Kept the prison. And here, an
 ANGEL awoke peter, by striking
The side and saying, Arise
Prompt! chains
Melted off his hands. and
The angel said to him: Gird yourself
And your sandals. And he did so.
The angel said: envelop up your coat of, and
Follow me.
Peter went out and followed him, not knowing
That what was being done by the angel was
Real, and Imagine having a vision.
When they had passed the first
Guard, then the second, they came
At the iron gate leading to the city

And open up to itself
Before them. They left, and rewards
 In a street soon the Angel
 Left peter. Back to himself,
Peter said, I now see
So certain that the Lord has
Sent his angel, and that he has delivered me
To The hand of Herod and all that
The Jewish people were expecting.

Listen! Acts 16: 23-26:
- In the middle of the night, PAUL
And Silas were praying and singing
After that they were responsible for beatings.
They threw them in prison, asking the jailer to keep them safely.
The jailer, who received the order, threw them into the inner prison
And put the vines to the feet.

By the middle of the night and PAUL
Silas were praying and singing
Praise be to God, and the prisoners
Heard them. Suddenly there was
A great earthquake
So that the foundations of the prison
 were shaken at the point
 All doors opening
And links of all prisoners
Were broken.

Listen! Acts 21: 10-14:

- As we had been there
For more days, a prophet named
Agabus, down from Judea, and came
Find us. He took the belt
Of Paul, tied his hand and foot, and
Said, 'Thus says the Holy- Spirit:

The man who owns this belt
 the Jews will bind the same
To Jerusalem, and deliver
In the hands of pagans.
When we heard this, we
And all people of the place we prayed
Paul not to go to Jerusalem
Then he said, WHAT ARE YOU DOING
Weeping and breaking my
HEART? I am ready, not only
To be bound, but also to
TO DIE IN JERUSALEM FOR
THE NAME OF THE LORD JESUS. As
He did not let himself be persuaded, we
Did not keep telling him, and we said:
MAY THE WILL OF THE LORD
BE DONE!

Listen! Acts 14: 19-20:
- Then occurred to Antioch and
 icon the Jews who won the crowd
And who, having stoned Paul, the
Dragged out of town, thinking
He was dead." But the disciples
The surrounding, he got up and went
In the city. The next day he went
With Barnabas to Derbe.

My brother, my sister, the apostles' faith in the gospel Of Jesus Christ strengthens me every day to worship JESUS CHRIST, TO TALK OF HIS NAME!

I know you're wondering, so here on Earth, we will not be -in abundance -in wealth, -into elevation -into success, into progress into promotion,-into Celibrity, etc. ...

The Apostle Peter one day asked the same question to Jesus after Jesus showed them that we must accept the loss to enter the kingdom of heaven. Matthew 19: 27-30

Listen! Matthew 19: 27-30:
- Peter then said: Here, we have all
Left, and we have followed you, what
Will be our reward ? Jesus answered
"I tell you the truth, when
the son of man, in the renewing of all things, will seat on the
throne of his glory you whom follow me will also
sit on twelve thrones, judging the
twelve tribes of israel. and whosoever
that will be out, due to
my name, his brothers, or
sisters or father or mother
or his wife or his children
or lands

Or his houses, shall receive an
Hundredfold, and "Inherit
ETERNAL LIFE. Many of the early
Shall be last and many of the
Last shall be first.

Here Jesus shows that he who is willing to lose everything for his name, he will not lose it he will receive a hundredfold in this century and the glory on his future.
That is why you will see when ABRAHAM accepted to lose ISAAC, he did not lose him. Genesis 22: 1-24

Do not separate with your families, your father, your mother, your brothers, your sisters etc ... "the Separation the Lord Jesus spoke is:- Not imitate the evil that -your father does -Your mother does , -your brothers do, your sisters do, your cousins do – your aunts do, -your uncles do, -your friends do, -do not imitate the evil
Of your company, -of your husband's family,- evil of your country etc ...

The apostles of the Lord Jesus Christ were still in contact with their families.

Matthew 8: 14:
- Jesus went to the house of
Peter he saw his stepmother lying
And having a fever.

Matthew 20: 20:
- Then the mother of the son of Zebedee approached
  Jesus with his son, and worshiped him to apply.

Even Jesus Christ was with children of Mary, who has found favor from God and begat the Lord Jesus Christ by the power of the Holy Spirit. Luke 1: 26-35

Listen! Luke 1: 26-35: - In sixth month angel Gabriel
Was sent from God unto a city of
Galilee called Nazareth, to a virgin betrothed to a man
Of house of David, named JOSEPH. The virgin's name was
MARIE.

The angel came into her house and said
I greet you, the one GRACE
WAS MADE, THE LORD IS WITH
You: troubled by this greeting
 MARIE Wondering what
Could mean this greeting
The angel said: Fear not
Mary, for you have found favor
With God. and here, you will conceive and give
 birth to A SON "and you will give the name OF JESUS.
He will be Great and will be called "THE SON
Of MOST HIGH "AND THE LORD GOD
Will give him 'THE THRONE OF DAVID his
father "

"He will reign forever on the house
Of Jacob , and his reign shall be no end "
Mary said to the angel: "How
it will be done, because I do
not know the man? Angel
said: "the holy spirit will
come on you, and the power of
The Most High will cover you with his
shadow." that is why the
HOLY CHILD BORN
WILL BE CALLED "SON OF GOD."

For me, I would like to make the same testimony that the Lord Jesus made in regard of JOHN-BAPTISTE concerning Saint Mary! "Surely, among those born of women there has not appeared a woman bigger than Mary, and there will be none.

"The Lord Jesus Christ was the last king" OF ISRAEL and he does not have a successor! "
"The house of Jacob," is a place where men, women worship God in spirit and in truth "
- Hear the words of the servants of Satan:
Matthew 2: 2:
- Saying, Where is the king of the Jews who is
Born for we have seen his STAR
In the East and have come to worship Him

CAN WE WORSHIP GOD IN THE FORM OF IMAGE STATUE, ETC ...?

To feed your curiosity, read for me:
Deuteronomy 4: 15-16:
- For you did not see any
Picture the day when the LORD
Spoke to you into fire at Horeb

Be carefully on your souls
Lest you do not corrupt yourself and that you do not do a Graven image, a representation of
Some idol, the figure of a man
Or a woman ...

For all nations who worship the statues, the figure of man, the figure of a woman, the figure of an animal, the figure of a bird, figure fish, figure of an animal that creeps on the earth, sun, moon, stars for gods, learn that: "THE ONLY TRUE GOD IS THE GOD OF ABRAHAM, ISAAC AND JACOB.

The gods made with hands of men, we know their origin, they come from man!

The God who has not a representation is above all things, man does not know "his origin"

"stop worshipping gods made with hands of men, they are not" God.

"Blessed is he who worships the GOD OF ABRAHAM, ISAAC, AND JACOB! Because he will Judge all these kings (gods). Revelation 17: 12-14

keep these in your mind:

-* babylon the great: is the church of the devil, satan." the prostitute!

-* seven mountains: are seven churches of devil, satan

-* ten horns: are the gods of nations

-* the beast: is the church where satan dwells on earth! revelation 17: 3

-* the false prophet: is the impi, the other beast

-* the dragon: satan

Just as God sent His ONLY SON JESUS CHRIST to save the world, the devil, Satan will also send his son to seduce the inhabitants of the earth. The other beast." Revelation 13: 11-12.

Revelation 13: 11-12:
- I saw a rise from the earth
Another beast, which had two horns
Similar to those of a "lamb
And spoke like a "dragon"
It exercises all the authority of the
First beast in his presence, and
She made the earth and its inhabitants-
Both worship the first beast
Whose deadly wound was
Been cured. 2 THESSALONIANS
2: 8-10

2 Thessalonians 2: 8-10:
 - And then will appear the ungodly, that
the Lord Jesus will destroy by
breath of his mouth, and he will
destroy by the brightness of his coming.

The coming of the IMPI will be by
Power of Satan, with all kinds of
Miracles, signs and marvels of iniquity
to seduce those who die because they have not
Received the love of the truth to be saved.

Many Jews have not believed in the birth of Christ "and through this hardening the devil, satan will introduce his son" to proclaim himself Christ "and he will seduce the nations!
2THESSALONICIENS 2: 3

2 Thessalonians 2: 3: let no one deceive you anyway; so, he must come The APOS-
TASIE before, and that
We may seen the man of sin
The son of "perdition,

The opponent who rises above
Of all that is called God until to sit
In the temple of God, to proclaim
himself GOD.

WHO ARE THE SEED OF ABRAHAM, ISAAC AND JACOB?

Listen! Genesis 12: 1-3:
- The Lord said to Abraham:
Leave your country, your homeland
And your father house
Into land I will show you
I will make you a great nation
I will bless you and I will make your name
Great, and you will be a source of
Blessing. I will bless those who
Bless you,

And all peoples on earth
Will be blessed through you.

My brother, my sister the good news is that everyone who receives the Lord Jesus Christ :- AFRICAN - AMERICAN - EUROPEAN,-OCEAN - ASIAN automatically becomes SON OF ABRAHAM, ISAAC, AND JACOB, because he has received The God who appeared to Abram and his descendants to bear his name for ever and ever.

THE BLOOD OF THE LORD JESUS CHRIST makes us JEWS . WATCH OUT! Do not limit yourself to be Jews only, but you also have to be born again to be agreed at table with ABRAHAM, ISAAC, AND JACOB.

HOW DOES ONE BORN AGAIN?

You must modify the law and live in The GOSPEL OF LOVE AND FORGIVENESS!
The Lord JESUS did not come to abolish the law but rather to correct (modify)!

Listen to this:-When God established MOSES and gave Him the law, God corrected some ways of man.

For instance: - before MOSES, incest "was not sin. When Moses came, God will say
that incest is sin "
"allow me to say that by
what we call incest, God
filled earth "

I gave you this example to show you that God has the power to modify His law"

Even the great Prophet of God "MOSES," spoke about the Lord JESUS. Acts 3:22-23

ACTS 3: 22-23:
- Moses said the Lord your God will raise up among your brothers A PROPHET LIKE ME, you listen to Him in everything HE TELLS YOU, and whoever will not hear that prophet shall be destroyed among people.

God sent His ONLY SON so that we develop love each other!
THE LAW does not teach us forgiveness, but grace tells us to forgive when somebody hurts you, but the law says: - Eye for eye, tooth for a tooth!
-THE LAW SAYS: - you shall not kill, the man who kills deserves to be punished by the judges!

-**GRACE SAYS**:-Anyone who gets angry against his brother deserves to be punished by the judges!
And whoever says to his brother, RICA! deserve
To be punished by the Sanhedrin, and that
Who will say 'You fool! Deserves to be punished by
The fire of hell!
-**THE LAW SAYS**-He who divorces his wife gives him a
Letter of divorce.
-**GRACE SAYS**: - Whoever divorces his wife, except for
Cause of infidelity expose her, to become adultery
And whoever marries a divorced woman

Commits adultery.

(Note: **more details will be found in the speech of akini: "we are like God**

for knowledge of live"

GRACE battle with sin in thought, in the Heart! It is By thinking of the evil that man commits sin, evil to his neighbor.

-**THE LAW SAYS**: - Do not commit adultery and ordered to kill adulterers. -Leviticus 20: 10

GRACE FORGIVE ADULTERERS. John 8: 1-11

Listen! John 8: 1-11: - Jesus went to the mountain
Of Olives. But in the morning he went again
In the temple, and all the people came to him.
Being seated, he taught them. Then scribles
And the Pharisees brought a woman-
Caught in the act, of adultery;

And, placing her among the people, they said
To Jesus, "Master this woman was taken
In the act of adultery. MOSES in the
LAW, commanded us to stone
WOMEN AS "so, what do you say?
They said that to seek a way
 To accuse Him. But JESUS! Having fallen
 He wrote with his finger on the ground. As
They continued asking him, he rose
And said: **LET ANYONE OF YOU
WITHOUT SIN CAST FIRST STONE
AGAINST HER**. And again declined
He wrote on ground when they heard
It, being convicted by their conscience, they are reticent
one by one, beginning at the eldest to the
Last;

And Jesus was left alone with the woman who was
There in the middle. Then stood up his head ,and no one was
there except the woman, Jesus said:
Woman, where are those accusers?
No one has condemned you? She
Said: No one, Lord. And Jesus said:
I do not condemn you either, go and
Do not sin again "
(NB: DO NOT MISS THE SPEECH OF AKINI)

WHAT SURPRISES ME IN THIS STORY, IS THE ABSCENCE OF THE MAN WITH WHO SHE HAD COMMITTED ADULTERY.!

Listen! Leviticus 20:10:
- If a man commits an adultery with a married woman,
If he commits adultery with the wife of his neighbor, the Man
"and Woman "

Adulterers will be put to death.

DEUTERENOME 10:22 :
-If we find a man sleeping with a married woman, they will die both, the man "who has slept
With the woman and the woman too.
You shall purge the evil into middle
OF ISRAEL "

* The Law of Moses "**orders to kill both! and where was the adultery man?**

 Man does not forgive the adultery of the wife but he wants the woman to forgive his adultery! And why this MAN?
The Lord JESUS CHRIST showed us how we must pray!
Matthew 6: 9-15:-here is how we should pray:

-Our father who is in heaven! Hallowed be thy name, your kingdom come, Thy will be done on earth as in heaven.

Give us every day our daily bread;
"Forgive us our trespasses, as we also forgive those who trespass against us, lead us not into temptation, but deliver us from evil for it is to you that belongs in every age, the kingdom, the power and glory. AMEN!

If you forgive men their trespasses, your father in heaven will also forgive you but if you do not forgive men their trespasses, your father will not also forgive you your trespasses.

*- *can you do this prayer? if yes! can you forgive "the adultery" of your wife?*

* why do you not pray the way the Lorr Jesus showed us ?

*he who is capable of doing this prayer is the one who can forgive in whatever state! " when you become able to forgive "sin whatever its state, then you can do" the prayer the Lord Jesus showed us "

* Never disregard it for **THIS PRAYER IS THE KEY OF LIFE "and never be HAPPY WHILE YOU ARE UNABLE TO DO IT".**

*** woman can you forgive your sister who has committed adultery with your husband?**

*** woman can you forgive your friend who has committed adultery with your husband?**

*** man can you forgive your brother who has committed adultery with your wife?**

*** man can you forgive your friend who has committed adultery with your wife?**

listen! Forgiveness is the Life of God, if we say we are God's children, let be ready to forgive sin, whatever its condition.

*** *can you forgive your mother*** (your father, your sister, your brother, your nephew, your niece, your cousin, your aunt, your uncle) ***magician one or witch, the one was the cause of the accident that*** killed your wife and your children?

*** *can you forgive*** the person who killed your husband?

*** *can you forgive*** the person who killed your child?

*** *can you forgive*** the one who killed your mother?

* *can you forgive* the one killed your father?

* **can you forgive** the one who killed your sister?

* *can you forgive* the one who killed your brother?

* *can you forgive* the one killed your niece?

* *can you forgive* the person who killed your cousin, your uncle, your aunt etc.

"*can you forgive* the one who poisoned you?

* *can you forgive* him who has transmitted AIDS to you?

* *can you forgive* the one defrauded you?

* *can you forgive* the one made a false accusation against you?

* *can you forgive* the one has made you blind, lame, weak?

* *can you forgive* the one who infirmed you?

* *can you forgive sin whatever its condition*?

* **THE LORD JESUS SAID**: Matthew 5:39:
 - But I tell you not to
Resist evil. If someone
 Strikes you on the right cheek, presente him the other also.
THE LORD JESUS teaches us to endure the pain! Be prepared to endure more pain caused by men!
If you forgive men's sins, forgiveness also will speak for you when you are in difficult times!

FORGIVENESS WILL SAY:- FATHER! FORGIVE him, as he always forgive others!

FATHER! Heal her daughter for she loves her neigbour

FATHER! Prosper his business for love lives in his heart!

FATHER! Give him this promotion for he keeps our love.

FATHER! Let him be Victorious in everything because he is led by love.

* If you can forgive sins that others can not forgive, ***CONSIDER YOURSELF AS GOD "AND*** The Lord JESUS will testify you to his Father, and HE and HIS Father shall dwell in you!

* FORGIVENESS IS THE SECRET OF THE GREAT POWER OF GOD *

LISTEN! MARC 11: 12-26:
 - The next day, after which they were come from Bethany he was hungry. seeing a fig tree afar off having leaves, he went to see if he could find something, and he approached, he found nothing but leaves, because it was not the season for figs. Then taking the word, he said, that no one ever eat fruit from you! And his disciples heard it. They came to Jerusalem, Jesus entered the temple. He began to cast out them that sold and bought in the temple, and overthrew the tables of the moneychangers and the seats of those selling doves, and he did not allow anyone to carry anything through the temple.

And he taught and said is it not written, My house shall be called a house of prayer for all nations?

But ye have made it a den of thieves. Pricipals priests scribles heard it, were looking a way to kill him: for they feared him, because the whole crowd was astonished at his doctrine when evening came, Jesus left the city. In the morning, by the way, they saw the Figs Dried to the roots.

Peter remembered what had happened said to Jesus, "Rabbi, look, THE FIGS you cursed has dried.

JESUS spoke, and said: Have faith in God " I tell you the truth if some one says to this mountain: "Stand up and throw yourself into the sea" and if he does not doubt in his heart but believes that what he said happens He will see it. That's why I tell you everything you ask for in prayer believe that you have received, and it will be yours. And when you're stand praying, IF YOU HAVE SOMETHING against anyone, **_FORGIVE, SO THAT YOUR FATHER WHO IS IN HEAVEN MAY FORGIVE YOU YOUR TRESPASSES._**

But if you do not forgive, your Father in heaven will not forgive you your trespasses.

* The disciples were amazed to see nothing but the word dried up roots figs tree ! But the Lord Jesus answered them: - when you stand to do *a prayer of faith "if you do not forgive the thing you have against anyone, God does not also hear you.*
* The Lord Jesus had mentioned pardon to teach us that faith without LIFE OF FORGIVENESS IS DEAD. "And when we forgive, God will also respond to our prayer of faith.

* THEN, we will pray for -the Blinds and they will see, we will pray for -the Deaf and they will hear, we will pray -for dumb and they will speak, we will pray -for the impotent And they will walk, we will pray- for the sick and they will be healed, we will pray- for sterile and they will be pregnant, we will pray -for witches, magicians, fetishists, those practices prohibited and they will be delivered,etc...

The Church has became a den of thieves!

Most of churches exist today, not **to do the work of God,** teaches its members the true way of God but rather to TRADE!

-The keys verses of those churches, are where God speaks of giving to his work and his servants!

* The worker deserves his wages! You have the right to eat for your work! But the Lord Jesus taught us one thing before leaving his disciples, that he who is in charge of the other has duty to wash the feet of its members.

- *DO YOU WASH THE FEET OF ORPHANS?*
-DO YOU WASH THE FEET OF WIDOWS?
***-DO YOU WASH THE FEET OF THE OPPRESSED*?**

Widows, orphans, the oppressed are ignored in many churches. PASTORS want church to care for them and their home.

God is the God of orphans, widows, the oppressed,
* THE POWER OF GOD IS NOT SHOWN IN MANY CHURCHES BECAUSE

Orphans and widows, the oppressed ... are neglected!
Isaiah 1:15-18:
- When you spread forth your hands I will hide
My eyes from you; when multiplied
Prayers, I will not listen, your hands are
Full of blood. Wash, purify you,
Remove from my eyes the wickedness
Of your actions, cease to do evil.
Learn to do good, search for jus-
Tice, protect the oppressed grants
The fatherless, the widow.
Come and plead now, SAYS THE LORD!.
Though your sins be as scarlet,
They shall be white as snow;
Though they be red like crimson, they
Become like wool.

If you have the good will and if
You are obedient, you shall eat the
Goods of the land, but if
You resist and you are rebels
You shall be devoured with the sword, because
THE MOUTH OF THE LORD has spoken.

Men of God, the mouth of the LORD has spoken. If you were neglected orphans, widows, the oppressed begin to be their hand.

God is their God and the church you direct is for God of the fatherless, the widow, the oppressed ...

You who listen to me, is a duty for all Of us! "Bless the oppressed, the orphans, the widows and" the windows of heaven will be open for you"

HE WHO LOVES IS READY TO DIE!

LISTEN! JOHN 15:12-13: -
This is my commandment:

-Do love one another as I have
Loved you. There is no greater love than a gifted
 His life for his friends. "

* ***LOVE HAS NO LIMITS!***
* ***LOVE FORGIVES!***
* ***LOVE SACRIFIES ITSELF!***

listen! god was looking for someone, who will agree to suffer without cause. "to be condanmed without case. "to be kill without cause and be a perfect model to the world concerning
Obedience to God. And no one in heaven or
On earth, or under the earth, was found worthy?

*and the only son of God has agreed to
stripped of all his glory next to
 his father and be born as a man
to suffer without raison, to be condanmed
without cause and dying without cause to
"save humanity who where suffering of death caused by
"adam!"*

It was through the disobedience of one man that the world has been CORRUPTED, so by the obedience of a man, the world is SAVED!
GOD DID NOT EXCEPT HIS ONLY SON, and gave Him to the world that whoever believes in Him, His teachings, should not perish, but have everlasting life.
The Lord Jesus Christ should be our model as Christians, we must sacrifice ourselves for others!
We must remain steadfast in faith in the Lors Jesus Christ through persecution, disease, suffering and torment, in tears to be a model for those who come to the Lord Jesus. **THE LORD JESUS HIMSELF IS OUR MODEL FOR THOSE WHO COME TO GOD.**

CAN WE EXCERCISE SOME OF PRACTICES OF LAW?

-The Lord Jesus said I am not come to abolish the law or the prophets but to accomplish it.
God in the law was using animals and birds and their blood, for sacrifices, but in grace, God uses the body of the Lord Jesus and His blood for our sacrifices.

LUKE 22:14-20:
The hour was come, he sat down with his
Apostles .He told them I wanted
 to eat this Passover with you
Before I suffer: for I say unto you, I won't
Eat it, until Fulfilled in the kingdom of God.
And he took the cup, gave thanks and
He said take this cup, and shared between
You, for I tell you, I will not drink
Of the fruit of the vine, until
That the kingdom of God comes.

And he took bread, and after giving
Thanks, he broke it and gave it to them, saying:
this is my body, which makes
For you do this in remembrance "
Of ME ". Likewise also the cup after
Dinner, and gave them, saying:
**this cup is the new covenant
in my blood** "which is shed for YOU.

* Understand that the body of the Lord Jesus which is the bread and blood of the Lord Jesus which is the wine took place directly of animals, birds and their bloods for:

- GUILT OFFERING!

-SIN OFFERING!

-THANKSGIVING OFFERING

-ALL CEREMONIES THAT REQUIRED ANIMALS, BIRDS AND THEIR BLOODS

-the consecration of the priests
-on the purification of leprosy

* the meal of the Lord is the formula that God"give us today!

give me your heart and listen now:

* the sin offering, the guilt offering were prepared for a category OF SINS.

LISTEN! - The deliverance of a sorcerer, a magician
The one who invokes spirit of a dead,
Those who practice taboos can not be performed the same
Way as the one of a thief, a liar, etc. ..

The deliverance of a possessed person can
 Not be performed the same as that of a
Arrogant man etc ..

Listen! Mark 9: 14-29:
 - When they came near
Disciples, they saw around them a great crowd
Scribles and arguing with them.

When the crowd saw Jesus, she was surprised, and ran to greet him. He asked them: what are you discussing with them? And a man of the crowd answered him, Teacher, I brought unto thee my son, who is possessed of a dumb spirit. Wherever he begins, he throws him on the floor, the child foam, grinds his teeth and becomes stiff. I asked your disciples to drive out the spirit, and they could not. Race unbelievers, Jesus said to them, how long will I be with you? How long shall I support you? Bring him to me. He was brought to him. and as soon as he saw him, the violent spirit shaked him, he fell to the ground and rolling in crying. JESUS asked his father, how is there time this has happened? Since childhood, he said. And often the spirit was thrown into the fire and water to destroy him. But if you can do anything, come to our aid, have compassion on us. Jesus: if you can! ...
All things are possible to him who believes. immediately the father of the child cried I beleive ! Help thou my unbelief!

Jesus saw the crowd rush, rebuked the unclean spirit, and said, dumb and deaf spirit, I command you, come out of him, and do not rent more. And he went, shouting and shaking him with great violence.

The child became as dead, so that many said he was dead. But Jesus, took him by the hand, lifted him up. And he stood. When Jesus came into the house, his disciples asked him privately, Why have we been able to drive it out? He told them:

* Then this sort can only come through prayer *

Matthew 17: 21:
- but this kind of demon come out only
Through prayer and fasting.

* Sorcerers, magicians, witchdoctors are servants of Satan after been into the table of demons, and "they must also come at the table of the Lord Jesus to be born again"

- **"they must eat the body of the Jesus and drink his blood which is the meal of lord.**

*** the meal of the lord will be for them atonement of sins and transmission of power of God***

*** a man who killed someone has the spirit of that man in him and he must go " partake to lord's meal" to atone his sin."**

* He who committed adultery has **the spirit of death in him** because the law condemns to death the adultery. He must go through "**the meal of lord for the atonement of his sin.**

"The sins we commit after having received the Lord Jesus must they be not atoned?"
The Lord Jesus did not come to abolish the law neither the prophets, so you will see that when the Lord Jesus healed a Leprous, he said to him go show yourself to the priest for the offering that **MOSES COMMANDED**, to be for them a testimony .Matthew 8: 1-4

what testimony?

-        *That the Lord Jesus did not come to ignore moses"(this was before the institution of the meal of the lord. today the offering of cleaning is done by the meal of the Lord)*

"the Lord Jesus, moses and elijah met all 3 to show us that all 3 make the institutions of God, and the Lord Jesus left alone to show us those 3   are summarized in "1" in "Jesus"

When you partake in the blood and flesh of the Lord Jesus by the "Meal of the Lord," Death is destroyed and the one with the power of death *satan is also* brought to nothing ". HEUBREUX 2: 14

"The Meal of the Lord" destroy the power of demons, evil spirits in the life of one who eats it!
"The Meal of the Lord"destroy the power of witches, magicians, witchdoctors, etc ... in the life of one who eats it!

"When a sorcerer, magician, etc ... eat the Meal of the Lord" he strips himself of his power and if he does not repent soon, have shamefully eating the body of Christ, he will be brought to trial against himself, he can become infirm, sick and even die. *this is why you will see sudden death. then, when a sorcerer , a magician eats the supper of the lord after repentance, the body and blood of the Jesus christ cast out the body and blood of satan in him.*

"when an adulterer eats the body of the Lord Jesus and drinks his blood after repentance, the blood and the body of the Lord Jesus cast out death in him because there is remission of sin trough the blood!

* God also spoke of sacrifice about restitution for wrongs! *

LISTEN! LEVITICUS 5: 20-26:
The Lord spoke to Moses, and
Said: If anyone sins and commits a trespass against the LORD in his next about a deposit, an object in his custody, a lost thing, or making a false oath on any thing that may constitute a sin and when sin and is guilty, he shall restore the thing he has stolen through fraud or subtract, the thing that was entrusted to him on deposit, the thing that he has lost found, or any thing on which he made a false oath.
He shall return in its entirety, will add fifth and return it to its owner, the day he will sacrifice his guilt offering. He will present to the priest as a sacrifice of guilty to the Lord for his sin a ram without blemish from the flock of your estimation. after the priest shall make atonement for him before the LORD and he will be forgiven, some is the fault of which he is guilty.

-Many people have cheated people, and after filling their pockets, they run faster in churches to become members and show people that they have changed and abandoned their evil deeds!

-Listen to me, hypocrites! it is not those who say
LORD! LORD! That will come in the kingdom of heaven, only those who do the will of God.
MATTHEW 7:21

-The will of God is that we worship him in Spirit and in Truth! You can not deceive God, what a man sows, he shall reaps. If you sow good, you shall reap peace and if you sow evil, you reap disorder. Galatians 6:7

Now is time you need to repent, those you have defrauded are there, you know them, and goods you have come from those people, help yourself with what you have, pay your debts and God will forgive you.
Even if you will sell your properties, sell them to be exempt before God, Satan and man!

* If you do not know, Satan is a great prosecutor, he will expose you himself before God and he will benefit through this door to make your life very miserable.

* All suffering are not the baptism of fire, there are also suffering in the Lake of Fire. "Matthew 3: 12

- the Lord Jesus told a rich man to sell all his items and follow him!

Listen! Matthew 19: 16-26:
 - And, behold, a man near by and said to him, Master, What should I do good to have eternal life? He answered: why do you question me on what is good? One is good. If you want to enter into life, keep the commandments. Which? He said. And Jesus answered, you shall not kill, thou shall not steal, Do not bear false witness, Honor your father and your mother and you shall love your neighbor as yourself, the young man said, I have observed all these things then! what else?
JESUS said: If you want to be perfect, go, sell what you possess, give to the poor and you shall have treasure in heaven.

Then come, follow me. After hearing these words the young man went away sorrowful, for he had great goods. JESUS told his disciples: I tell you the truth, a rich shall hardly enter into the kingdom of heaven.
I tell you again, it is easier for a camel to go through the eye of a needle than a rich man to enter the kingdom of God. The disciples heard it were amazed and said that then who can be saved?
Jesus looked at them and said, "With men this is impossible but with God all things are possible.

the Lord Jesus is not the God of poors, he does not seek to be surrounded by poors. "gold and silver belong to him.

This rich man, is like you, you observe the laws of God, you are no longer walking the walk as a pagan, but you have to do one thing, pay **your DEBT EVEN IF** you must be **excluded from the ranks of rich and you'll be everywhere with the Lord Jesus"**

-and the good news for all of you who agree to lose, will gain in hundredfold things they accepted to lose because of the Lord Jesus Christ.

IN A CASE THERE IS NO ONE TO RETURN?

LISTEN! NUMBER 5: 5-10:
- The Lord spoke to Moses, and said, speaking to the Israelites: When a man or woman sin against his neighbor by committing a trespass in respect of the Lord. And he will be found guilty, he will confess his sin, and will return its ill-gotten gains around the object in 'adding fifth, he hand to him to whom he was guilty***! IF THERE IS ONE WHO HAS THE RIGHT TO A REFUND OF THE SUBJECT*** ill-gotten gains, this object returns to the LORD, to the priest also the ram with which atonement shall be made for the guilty. Any offering of holy things that the children of Israel will presented belongs to the priest . The things that will be delivered belong to.

"THE PRIEST IS THE ONLY ONE GOD" LAID TO TAKE RESTITUTION FOR WRONGS GAINS WHEN THERE IS NO ONE.

WHAT IF THE PERSON IS UNABLE TO PAY THE WHOLE ILL-GOTTEN GAINS?

God is love, that's why Jesus said:
- come to me, all of you who are weary and burdened.

Take my yoke upon you and learn from me, for I am gentle and lowly in heart: and you shall find rest for your souls.
The priest (pastor) will tax him, and will estimate related to the resources of this man. LEVITQUE: 27: 8

WHAT TO DO REGARDING THE ONE WHO GOT HIS WEALTH BY MAGIC, FETISH, ETC ..?

He must also make "restitution of his goods but in this case, he will do it by the act of redemption. **the priest will tax him with the help of the holy spirit, and money he will bring must be applied for the work of the church, and this will be a memorial to the Lord for the redemption of its properties. (- you can buy a land for the church, the tools of the church, what you will do with that money should be for the church of God)**

Pastor, it is not your money to buy a car, a house, etc ...*

The devil who was the source of that wealth will claim his wealth and The Angel of God will show him the land purchased for the church, etc ... and the devil will be unable to claim because **the church of christ walk on him but when the angel shows your car, house, etc ... you have to expect disaster because it belongs to him.**

Let's not be greedy! GOD has a salary for servants who fear him!

* ***AFTER THE ACT OF REDEMPTION***, he must partake at the "The table of the Lord"for atonement of sin.

* The one who received his wealth through prostitution should also do the act of redemption "and partake to "the meal of the Lord" for atonement of her sins. Here the priest may use the money: it's the same case with the ill-gotten gains. NUMBER 5: 5-10

Anyone who made his pocket by stealing, by diversion is in the same case of ill-gotten gains.

THE IMPACT OF THE MEAL OF THE LORD

Many people eat the meal of the Lord without understanding its impact into the life of a person!

Listen! 1 corinthians 11: 23-34:
- For I have received from the Lord what I taught you: that the Lord Jesus in the night he was handed over, took bread and gave thanks, broke it and said this is my body which is broken for you: do this in remembrance of me. Likewise, after supper he took the cup, saying, This cup is the new covenant in my blood, every time you will drink whenever you eat this bread and drink this cup, you proclaim the Lord's death until he comes.
Therefore whoever eats the bread or drinks the cup of the Lord unworthily will be guilty of the flesh and blood of the Lord. Let a man examine himself, and so eat the bread and drink of the cup, for he who eats and drinks without discerning "the Lord's body,eats and drinks judgment against himself. That's why there are many among you are weak and sick, and many died. If we judge ourselves, we should not be judged, but when we are judged, we are chastened of the Lord, that we should not be condemned with the world. So, my brothers, when you come together for dinner, wait for one another.

If someone is hungry, let him eats at home, so you do not come together to draw judgments about you and I deal with other things when I come.

The first message I heard from my spiritual father Richard N' konji was on "***the meal of the Lord. i was very frightened, by listening to his teaching and i have promised myself that i will not eat "the meal of the Lord even if they offer me. Since i met Christ -in july 1995" the meal of the Lord became my very, very, very admirable food ... because every time i eat, christ developes in me* ".**

* in the meal of the Lordman eats the body of Jesus christ "and drink the blood of Jesus christ"

what is the impact of the body of Jesus christ?

***listen*!** JOHN 3: 14-16:
- And as Moses lifted "the serpent in the desert, likewise **THE SON OF MAN** may be lifted whoever believes in him has **"ETERNAL LIFE.** For God so loved the world that He gave His **ONLY SON**, that whoever believes in him should not perish but have everlasting life. "

LISTEN! NUMBER 21: 1-9:
-The king of Canaanite Arad, who dwelt in the south, heard that Israel came by way of atharim. He fought Israel, and took prisoners. However Israel made a vow to the Lord and said, if you deliver this people into my hands, I will devote its cities to destruction. The LORD heard the voice of Israel, and delivered up the Canaanites. They are utterly destroyed them and their cities, and they named the place Hormah. They traveled from Mount Hor by the way of the Red Sea, to turn the land of Edom. The people grew impatient on the road, and spoke against God and against Moses, why have you up out of Egypt, for we die in the desert?
Because there is no bread, and there is no water, and our souls are disgusted with this wretched food. So the LORD sent against the people fiery serpents, and they bit the people, and many people died in Israel. The people came to Moses, saying: we have sinned, for we have spoken against the LORD and against you. Requests the LORD, that he takes away the serpents from us. Moses prayed for the people "The Lord said to Moses: - Make thee a fiery serpent, and set it upon a pole, anyone who is bitten, and looked at it, shall live. Moses made a bronze serpent, and places it on a pole, and whoever had been bitten by a snake and looked at the bronze serpent, he lived.

-The body of the Lord Jesus symbolizes "**THE DEATH OF The Lord JESUS.**"

-Through body of the Lord Jesus there is life for humanity "the body of the Lord Jesus delivers **MAN FROM DEATH**", the one who "eata the body of the Lord Jesus eats healing for his problem."

* THE ONE WHO BELIEVES THAT The BODY The DEATH OF The Lord JESUS Deliver from DEATH, HAS EVERLASTING LIFE ".

That's why the Lord Jesus said: "HE WILL BE LIFTED, and ANYONE who believes in his death will have eternal life." Whoever confesses that the death "of the Lord Jesus gives life, God directly releases *"HEALING INTO HIS LIFE "*

* My brother, my sister, the prayer of faith will push God to release miracles in your life! So when you pray, talk **with assurance that the death of the Lord Jesus is life for your problems.**

THIS IS HOW TO PRAY: - Son of the living God
Lord Jesus Christ, I beleive your death gives life to all my problems, because God has given us your death "for the healing of our problems, whatever their severity. I beleive your death gives life to the lungs.

God Will Release his healing when you testify with confidence upon death of the Lord Jesus.
   ANY ONE WHO HONORS The LORD JESUS, GOD WILL ALSO HONOR HIM AS WELL "

God acts only through the Lord Jesus "and without the Lord Jesus there is no salvation, healing, miracles from God of Abraham, Isaac, and Jacob.

**- i beleive your death Lord Jesus gives life to the heart, i want to say that your death heals ...... 7 times (tell your heart disease) .*

**- i beleive your death Lord Jesus gives life in the blood, i want to say that your death heals ...... 7 times (tell your blood disease).*

**- i beleive your death Lord Jesus gives life to the flesh, i want to say that your death heals ...... 7 times(tell the skin disease that you have).*

**- i beleive your death Lord Jesus gives life to toe, i mean your death consolidate feet: "get up in the name of Jesus christ. 7 times.*

**- i beleive your death Lord Jesus gives life to the eyes, i want to say that your death opens eyes of blind: "open your eyes and see in the name of Jesus christ." 7 times*

*- i beleive your death Lord Jesus gives life to the ears, i want to say that your death opens ears "listens and hears in the name of Jesus christ"...   7 times

*- i beleive your death Lord gives life to the mouth, i mean that your death opens mouth: "open your mouth and speak in the name of Jesus christ ..." 7 times

*- i beleive your death Lord Jesus gives life to any disability, i mean that your dead Jesus gives strength to paralytic, "get up on your bed in the name of jesus christ .. .. "7 times
*- i beleive your death Lord Jesus heals all kinds of diseases, i mean your death cure aids "let your blood be pure in the name of Jesus-christ and go for exam ...... 7 times

*- i beleive your death Lord Jesus gives life to all kinds of diseases, i mean that your death Jesus heals cancer in all its names: "be healed in the name of Jesus christ and va examine you." .....7 times
*- i beleive your dead lord jesus gives life to all kinds of diseases, i mean that your dead jesus heals the diabetes: "be healed in the name of jesus christ and go for exam." .... 7 times

*- i beleive your death Lord Jesus gives life to bones, i mean that your death Jesus heals all diseases of bones: "be healed in the name of Jesus christ "........ 7 times

*- i beleive your death lord Jesus gives life to matrix, i mean that your death Jesus gives children to a sterile woman conceive in the name of Jesus christ ...... 7 times

*- i beleive your death lord Jesus gives promotion: "receive the promotion in the name of Jesus christ .... 7 times

*- i believe your death Lord Jesus gives prosperity: "receive the success in the name of Jesus christ ..... 7 times

*- i beleive your death lord Jesus makes rich "receive wealth in the name of Jesus christ "..... 7 times

*- i beleive your death lord Jesus makes victorious "receive victory in all your business in the name of Jesus christ "..... 7 times

*- i beleive your death Lord Jesus makes grown body parts cut ...... 7 times: let your body grow in the name of the Lord Jesus christ, who created man by his own hands when even a body part of man did not exist. everything is possible for him who believes.

* May the God who appeared to me in the fire to write you his words, testify his word in your life by healinga, miracles, wonders, great signs, etc ...

*You can use the death of the Lord Jesus to pray for someone else. A firm insurance gives rise to a TESTIMONY! "

WHAT IS THE IMPACT OF THE BLOOD OF THE LORD JESUS CHRIST?

The blood symbolizes life! The blood of the Lord Jesus Christ symbolizes **LIFE OF THE LORD JESUS- CHRIST**.

* the body and blood of the Lord Jesus christ are "weapons of God for us to fight Satan, his demons, the gods of nations, sorcerers, magicians, witch doctors, all his kingdom for ever and ever ......

* the life of the Lord Jesus is the life of the redeemer! The Lord Jesus is the redeemer. So, when you drink blood of the Lord Jesus, you drink redemption of your life. "

* Trough the Blood of the Lord Jesus Christ "the file that condemn us to death is cleared.

* When Adam sinned against God, all the fruit of his womb were also sentenced to death – THAT IS THE FILE. Job 14: 4

* THE BLOOD OF THE LORD JESUS takes away the sins we have committed individually and inherited, it means blood makes them like they never been!

Understand that once you accept that THE BLOOD OF THE LORD JESUS CHRIST "takes away the sin, whatever its condition, directly the file of your sins are erased and the devil will be with no file" to accuse you before God.

* You will be free of conscience according to your **FAITH IN THE BLOOD OF THE LORD JESUS CHRIST "**

LISTEN TO ME MY CHILD! "It will be much forgiven to who Believes much in the work of the blood *of THE LORD JESUS CHRIST. "*

LISTEN TO ME MY FRIEND "- Moses was given for a single Nation, the descendants of Abraham, Isaac, and Jacob (in flesh) **TO TEACH THE WAY OF GOD**. We, Africans, Americans, Europeans, Asians, Oceanics were not called the people of God;

but God by his great love, he sent his only son Jesus christ (- only one means: he is the only one who has all the spirit of God in him) to make all the peoples of the earth people of God trough his blood and his blood makes us son of abraham, isaac, and jacob.

* Listen to the words of those who sit around God, revealed to the servant of the Lord Jesus Christ, John by the Angel of God. Revelation 5: 8-10.

Revelation 5: 8-10:-When he had taken the book, the four Living creatures and the twenty-four Old men fell down before the Lamb, each holding a harp and golden bowls full of incense, which are the prayers of saints. and they sang a new song, saying, Thou art worthy to take the book, AND to open its seals, for You were slain and hast redeemed us to God "with your blood" men from every tribe, and tongue , and people, and nation: thou hast made them a kingdom and priests to our God and they shall reign on Earth "

-the blood of the Lord Jesus christ "has the power to erase mark of perdition 666, the name of the beast on any person who accepts the Lord Jesus christ for his master" and lord. " listen to the mystery of the death of the Lord Jesus christ:
- when adam "sinned, he descended into dead places" that means his- life -family" –his descendants ", - his health", his joy, "all his best were down with him in the living dead!. and now it required someone to go down also to "bring back to life by his blood" man ", his life," his family, "his seed", his health, "joy", all the best of him!

and the body of Jesus christ "enabled Jesus to come down into residence of the dead, and the blood" of Jesus christ allowed him to bring back man to live , and all belongins " his life" his family "and his seed ",his health ", his joy," all the best of man.

Apply also the blood of the Lord Jesus christ when you pray, and have faith "in the blood that he revives, he brings back to life all things, and you will sing a new song:

: **"I HAD AIDS, AND THE BLOOD OF THE LORD JESUS PURIFIED MY BLOOD".**

* If you beleive a lot into the blood of the Lord Jesus Christ, you will also see many great things in your life!

THIS IS HOW TO PRAY: - ONLY SON OF THE LIVING GOD, LORD JESUS CHRIST, I believe that by your death you went down in the living dead to redeem with your blood "my life and my goods." I beleive your blood is approved by **GOD FOR BEVERAGE TO BRING TO LIFE, MY LIFE AND MY GOODS.**

*- i beleive your blood lord jesus christ heals and i apply it on my heart for his healing ....7 times (tell the disease of the heart you have)

*- i beleive your blood Lord Jesus christ heals, and i apply it on my lungs .... 7 times (tell the lung disease that you have)

*- i beleive your blood Lord Jesus christ purifies, and i apply it on my body to remove the mark of celibacy ..... 7 times

*- i beleive your blood, Lord Jesus christ delivers, and i apply it in my heart to uproot seed of the devil: jealousy-,- arrogance, lying, ,-greedyness, fornication, etc .... 7 times

*- i beleive your blood, Lord Jesus christ heals and i apply it into my blood to heal me of aids .... 7 times
*- i beleive your blood, Lord Jesus christ delivers and i apply it into my spirit to cut all ties of nightwedding .... 7 times

*- i beleive your blood Lord Jesus christ operates miracles and i apply it in my eyes to remove the scales: "open your eyes and see in the name of jesus christ ".... 7 times

*- i beleive your blood Lord Jesus christ operates miracles and i apply it to my ears to remove the scales of voicelessness ,"listen and hear in the name of the Lord Jesus christ ".... 7 times
*- i beleive your blood Lord Jesus christ operates miracles and i apply it to my mouth to remove the lock in the name of Jesus christ....... 7 times

*- i beleive your blood Lord Jesus christ operates miracles and i apply it on my feet to walk: "get up in the name of the Lord Jesus christ and walk "........ 7 times

*- i beleive your blood, lord Jesus christ operates miracles and i apply it on my body against paralysis, "and walk in the name of tahe Lord Jesus christ .... 7 times

*- i beleive your blood Lord Jesus christ heals and i apply it on my bones for healing ..... 7 times

*- i beleive your blood, Lord Jesus christ heals and i apply it to my womb for its recovery: "be fruitful in the name of the Lord Jesus christ .... 7 times

*- i beleive your blood Lord Jesus christ heals and i apply it on my flesh for his recovery ... 7 times

*- i beleive your blood, Lord Jesus christ heals and i apply it on me to be cured of cancer, diabetes, tuberculosis ... 7 times

*- i beleive your blood Lord Jesus christ prospers and i apply it into my hands to prosper in all things ..... 7 times

*- i beleive your blood Lord Jesus christ prospers and i apply it on my feet to walk from victory to victory .... 7 times

*- i beleive your blood Lord Jesus christ gives work and i apply it on my diplomas to find job ... 7 times

*- i beleive your blood Lord Jesus christ protects and i apply it on my car to prevent me against accident ..... 7 times

*- i beleive your blood Lord Jesus christ protects and i apply it on my house to prevent against thiefs .... 7 times

*- i beleive your blood Lord Jesus christ protects and i apply it on my children against bad friends.... 7 times

*- i beleive your blood Lord Jesus christ protects and i apply it on my wife against infidelity .... 7 times

*- i beleive your blood Lord Jesus christ protects and i apply it on my husband against infidelity, against murder etc ...

it is up to you to make sentences, while having a firm assurance that the blood of the Lord Jesus christ, redeems, secures, delivers, heals, etc ...

The body "and blood of the Lord Jesus Christ are the two weapons of God who reduced the devil, satan to zero.

" use always both weapons when you pray.

"the blood of the Lord Jesus christ has power to grow the limbs cut off."

* fear of God are aminissions of both two weapons! "the fear of God is to receive the Lord Jesus christ as our guide.

* There is only one person that God has testified in the mouth of Moses, the prophets, angels to serve as intermediate between God and men: "**IS THE LORD JESUS CHRIST**"

-The teachings of the Lord Jesus Christ are approved by God to be observe by men. Indeed, the Lord Jesus did not speak of himself, but he conveyed what the Father had commanded him to speak to the world. The Lord Jesus Christ came not to do his will but the will of him who sent him. Whoevet hears the Lord Jesus Christ, believes in the God of Abraham, Isaac, and Jacob. God has put all his authority in thr Lorr Jesus that is why the Lord Jesus said and says: Whoever has seen me, has seen the Father, the one who sees the father sees me. THE FATHER AND I ARE ONE "

I know you are shocked by listening to this as people who were with the Lord Jesus in the flesh! JOHN 14: 8-9.

Listen, Father has made himself equal to Jesus christ his son :
-the Father raises the dead and he gave also the Son power to raise the dead .

-the Father forgives sins and he gave the power also to the Son to forgive sins.
-the Father gives eternal life and gave also to the son the power to give eternal life.
"and again, he gave his 7 spirits of God, this is why he is called "only son". there is nothing that the father does the son can not do.
" he who honors the son, honors also the father", -one who recognizes the authority of the son ", recognizes the authority" of the father "-he who calls christ father, recognizes the father, as father.
* the one who does not believe that christ is equal to the father, denies the father .
* blessed those who believe that christ "is the father because" they will do the works the Lord Jesus christ has prrformed and they will do in large because he went to the father who is greater than him. "Jesus is the father".

I wonder when people say:-the greatest things that the Lord Jesus "spoke are" *INVASIONS "(TECHNOLOGY)*.

-UNBELIEVERS! -Do not you understand that "a bird is more than a plane - "a horse more than a Car "; a man more than a machine."

-The Lotd Jesus said he who believes in him will do the works that he has done and will do the greatest!. That is to say those who believe "- HE IS" FATHER "

* Scientiats who made these invasions,do they believe in "the Lord Jesus?" Do they beleive: "**THE LORD JESUS IS THE FATHER?"**

THE GREATEST: - It is to say more:
*- If he healed a thousand sick people,in HIS NAME we will heal more than one thousand.

 *-If he rose a dead after 4 days, in his name we will raise more than 4 days.

*- If he opened eyes of 2 thousands blinds, in his name we will open more than 2 thousands.

*- If he opened the ears of 3 thousands deaf, in his name we will open more than 3 thousands.

*- If opened mouth of 4 thousands, in his name we will open more than 4 thousands.

*- If he has made walked 5 thousands impotent, in his name we will perform over 5 thousands.

*- if he walked 100 meters on the sea ,in his name we will walk over 100metres.

Note: - there is not a greater miracle "which man can do with "the spirit of God that the Lord Jesus has not done.

"the world and all it contains were created by the Lord Jesus christ." john 1: 1-3

- man is more than the miracle of a part of body which grows"

- "Technology is not bad, it also helps us to preach" the Gospel of the Lord Jesus throughout the world, through television, radio, internet, Facebook,twitter ,cell Phone,etc..
* One day, someone asked me, "Pastor, invasions are the devil inspirations! I looked him and said - **LEARN THAT EVEN "THE DEVIL, SATAN SERVE THE LIVING GOD.**

So if technology comes from the devil, Satan, then "the devil is in" perseverance to serve the living God cause the gospel of "the Lord Jesus" is more easy to be heard!
I told him again: - "the devil, Satan served God in" killing the Lord Jesus Christ because God needed his death "to reconcile with man"

To finish with him, I said - "remember that God is the source of all intelligence, wisdom, knowledge"
A scientist is already very, very smart in the womb and "Where did all come from?.... **OF COURSE FROM GOD**"

back on the impact of the" meal of the lord" in the life of a person who eats it!

* he who eats "the meal of the Lord with a pure heart" announces the death of the Lord and the resurrection of the lord. "he announces that" the Lord Jesus christ is alive"

* He announces that the Lord Jesus Christ overcame the devil, satan, * he announces that the Lord Jesus Christ is at the "father's right hand , he announces that * **THE LORD JESUS CHRIST IS THE WAY, TRUTH AND LIFE**, * he announces that the Lord Jesus Christ has redeemed "all his life and his property." When you proclaim victory, you will see victory!

*- When you are defiled by sin and you eat "the meal of the Lord " know that "you are" guilty of the body and blood of the Lord ", you put yourself in" Judgement against yourself.

*- Examine yourself before eating the Lord's body and drinking his blood for fear that "you eat and drink the trial! That is why, you will see in churches people with incurable diseases, people who lose their body parts "by accident, people who become infirm, people die a lot!

LISTEN! We testify before satan,demons,gods of nations,magicians,sorcerers,witchdocters,... **THAT "THE LORD JESUS CHRIST IS ALIVE" BUT WHEN YOU SAY The LORD JESUS CHRIST IS ALIVE,** "they also need to see the Lord Jesus Christ in you. Then when he is not in you, "you are without protection, they quickly come torture you with" disease or infirmity,with problems to bring you to hate "the way of God or even kill you ! ACTS 19: 13-16

Life of sanctification is "money we pay to accommodate the Lord Jesus to dwell in us! JOHN 15:4

ONE WHO IS NOT BORN AGAIN, CAN NOT EAT "THE MEAL OF THE LORD!

* When you accept the gospel of the Lord Jesus Christ, then you must be baptized "***BY WATER AND SPIRIT. JOHN 3: 5***
THE BAPTISM OF WATER!

Listen! Matthew 3: 1-12: - in those days appeared John Baptist preaching in the wilderness of Judea. He said: Repent for the kingdom of heaven is near. JEAN is the one that was spoken by Isaiah the prophet, saying, this is the voice of one crying in the wilderness: Prepare the way of the Lord, make his paths straight. John was clothed with camel's hair and a leather belt around his waist. He ate locusts and wild honey. The inhabitants of Jerusalem, throughout Judea and across the country about Jordan, went out to him and confessing their sins, were baptized by him in the sea of Jordan. But come to his baptism seeing many of the Pharisees and Sadducees, he said, O generation of vipers, who hath warned you to flee from the wrath to come: Bring forth therefore fruits worthy of repentance, and think not to say to yourself;

We have Abraham as our father! " I tell you that from these stones God can raise up children to Abraham. " Already the ax is laid unto the root of the trees: therefore every tree which brings not forth good fruit is cut down and thrown into the fire. I baptize you with water, to bring you to repentance: but he that cometh after me is mightier than I, and I am not worthy to wear his shoes. Him, he will baptize you with the Holy Spirit and fire. He has his van to the hand, he thoroughly purges his floor and gathers his wheat into the barn, but he will burn the chaff with unquenchable fire.

* Water baptism is the baptism of repentance ", that is to say, man must make the decision to abandon his wicked ways," and live into the word of God "and once you are armed with this thought, that's when your water baptism is approved" by God and you now have access to the baptism of the Spirit.

* Many people are baptized without taking the decision to separate from evil as Pharisees and sadduciens. They believe that they get the "key of the kingdom of heaven by been baptised! They are baptised to deceive people that they have changed but they are still witches, magicians, they still practice forbidden !".......

* BAPTISM WITHOUT REPENTANCE IS VOID *

- "You can not deceive God, he put to open what is hidden in darkness, he put to light the shadow of death "
* You who is witch , magician , witchdoctor, you who practice banned etc. .... and you are "in the church of God, one calls you, Brother, Sister, servant of GOD, evangelist, pastor, apostle it is **TIME FOR YOU TO REPENT! " GOD LOVES YOU!**

-BE STRONG! Go to the man of God, tell him you are a sorcerer , or magician or witchdoctor or practices taboos so that you may be delivered from the bondage of the devil in **THE NAME OF THE LORD JESUS CHRIST !**
-Don 't be ashamed to confess your sins. There is no life in keeping a secret of your state.

- *"you who are sorcerer, magician, witch doctor or practices taboos (invoke the dead, the spirits etc ...) bring your evil books, your instruments of work to be burned by a person who has the anointing of God.*

Listen! Acts 19: 18-19: - many of those who believed
Came and confessed, and they declared what they had done. And
a number of those who had held the magical arts, having
brought their books and burned them before all the world: we
estimated the value to fifty thousand pieces of silver.

*- You who are sorcerer, take all your instruments of work and
bring them to the church to be burned.

*- you who are magician   bring all your books and your
instruments to the church to be burned.

*- You who are witchdoctor, bring all your work instruments to
the church to be burned.

While you listen to "the voice of God do not harden your heart! If
you do not want to repent, God will expose your person and you
will trample under foot of men. "Nothing hidden, will always
remain hidden"

*- You who are prostitute, thief, adultery, Criminal, etc ... **AND YOU ARE IN THE CHURCH OF GOD**, one call you "brother, sister, elder, deacon, deaconess, servant of god, evangelist, pastor, apostle, bishop, Servant of God, protocol," **TIME HAS COME FOR YOU TO REPENT! GOD LOVES YOU!**

CAN WE CONFESS OUR SINS TO A SERVANT OF GOD?

DEFINITELY YES! There are other sins you have committed need "only the priest to make sin offering (atonement) for you before God. Remember that the Lord Jesus Christ said: I came not to destroy the law "or the prophets." "Your confession of sins" allow "the man of God to know which spirits" to cast out during your deliverance. "

For insistance: -* YOU KILLED A PERSON, THE CHILDREN YOU HAVE, ARE NOT FOR YOUR HUSBAND, YOU ARE -* A SORCERER *- A MAGICIAN *- A WITCH DOCTOR; *- PRACTICE TABOOS; *- YOU SOLD YOUR SEED FOR MONEY;

- YOU DESTROYED A MATRIX OF A WOMAN *- YOU POISONNED SOMEONE, *- YOU STOLE FROM SOMEONE; *- YOU TRANSMITTED DISEASE WITH A CONSCIENCE TO SOMEONE ....

" God has established the Lord Jesus Christ, priest for all humanity and the Lord Jesus Christ established your pastor, priest on you "

Take courage! Go to man of God, tell him you are "a prostitute, a thief ", adultery, criminal etc. .... and THE BLOOD OF THE LORD JESUS CHRIST, you will take away your sins "
Happy! He who sets his eyes on the cross of The Lord Jesus Christ, because he will be saved from his sins.

THE BAPTISM OF HOLY SPIRIT!

LISTEN! JOHN 14: 18: - I will not leave you orphans
I shall come to you.

JOHN 14:26:-but the Comforter, **THE HOLY SPIRIT**
That the Father will send in my name will reveal you every things

And remind you all that I told you.

JOHN 15: 26:-when the Comforter comes that
I will send you from the FATHER
The Spirit of truth who proceeds from the Father
He will testify about me.

GOD SAID: I no longer live in houses made by human hands, I will live into man who is my temple. Your "body is became the temple of God after Baptism of WATER!" However, because you keep the word of God, the Lord Jesus Christ will make his home in you by the prescence of the Holy Spirit in you ".

The Holy Spirit in you will reveal you hidden things and future of your life ",about your family," the thing you do not know, "he will reveal the mysteries of God, he will reveal things .... .

The Holy Spirit in you, will make you wise among the Gentiles - he opens the mind, he gives knowledge, he opens eyes to see visions, dreams – he opens ears to hear oracles of God – he opens mouth to prophesy things to come. 6 DANIEL: DANIEL 3 1: 19-20 ACTS 10:38 ACTS 2:1-47

Trough The Holy Spirit in man that God works "healing" miracles "and wonders," great signs ....

Without the Holy Spirit, we can not do these things. That is why the Lord Jesus Christ said, without me you can not do anything. John 15: 5

* The Holy Spirit is **THE SPIRIT OF GOD OF THE LORD JESUS CHRIST!**

* ***HAPPY! ONE WHO IS PREPARED TO RECEIVE THE FATHER AND HIS SON, BECAUSE THEY WILL LET KNOWN BY HIM "***

LISTEN! I CONREITHIENS 2: 11-12:-which men, in fact knows the things of man except the spirit of man which is in him? Similarly, no one knows the things of God except the Spirit of God.
Now we have not received the spirit of the world, but the spirit that comes from God, that we might know the things that God has given us by his grace "

Life of holiness keeps "The Holy Spirit into man, and when man likes to defile, "demons who lived before, comes back into their home, this time with many. Matthew 12: 43-45

LISTEN! Matthew 12: 43-45:-when the unclean spirit goes out of a man, he walked through dry places, seeking rest, and if he found none. Then he said: I will return into my house whence I came out, and when he arrives, he finds it empty, swept, and ("-the abscence of the Holy Spirit) he goes, and takes with him seven other spirits more wicked than himself, they enter they dwell there, and the last state of that man is worse than the first. It will be the same for this wicked generation (those who do not keep the word of God ")

He who makes the decision to separate from evil, "one who really believes that **the LORD JESUS CHRIST HAS THE WORD OF LIFE" is directly "BAPTIZED IN THE SPIRIT BY GOD" OF BAPTISM OF WATER AND HE CAN BE " BAPTISED OF THE" HOLY SPIRIT "before moving on to WATER BAPTISM.**" ACTS 10: 44-48.

LISTEN! ACTS 11: 44-48:-While Peter yet spoke these words, the Holy Ghost fell on all who heard the word. All the circumcised believers who came with Peter were astonished "that the gift of the Holy Spirit had been poured on pagans .for they heard them speaking in tongues and glorifying God.
Then Peter said, can we forbid water "for baptizing these people who have received the Holy Ghost as well as we?

And he commanded them to be baptized in the name of the Lord. On what they asked him to stay a few days with them.

CIRCUMCISION THAT GIVES SALVATION!

GENESIS 17: 9-14: - God said to Abraham: you , you will keep my covenant, you and your seed after thee in their generations. This is my covenant, you shall keep, between me and you and your seed after you: every male among you shall be circumcised, your circumcision will be a sign of the covenant between me and you., At the age eight days every male among you shall be circumcised in your generations, whether born in the house, or bought with money of any foreigner son, not of your race. One must circumcise one born in the house and the one bought with money, and my covenant in your flesh will be an everlasting covenant. An uncircumcised male who is not circumcised in the flesh will be cut off from his people: he hath broken my covenant.

* GOD previously lived in houses made by human hands "but at this time of grace" **TIME OF HIS ONLY SON, JESUS CHRIST**, He no longer lives in houses made by human hands "

* That is to say, God before needed circumcision done by the hand of man "to accept a person and call him" his people "because it was**" THE MARK OF PERFECTION** ",
But in this time of grace, *time of his only son Jesus christ "he needs to see" the mark of perfection, the name of the only son of God "on the front of every one who wants to be called son of abraham , people of the living God. "*

* One who circumcises himself, does right thing before God, and whoever does not circumcise himself is not considered a sinner before God. But he who **has THE MARK OF PERFECTION , THE NAME OF THE ONLY SON OF GOD,** Jesus Christ on his forehead, is greater than that circumcised "flesh"

THE IMPACT OF THE BAPTISM OF FIRE!

Never be happy Christian, if you do not yet passed through the "baptism of fire". "glory comes after suffering!

My father Papa Richard always told me Dede, never be happy because you are not yet gone through fire. "I was not pleased listening to that

I was already suffering and what suffering to suffer again? ... My father was a great prophet of God!

Today my joy is perfect for the Spirit of God baptized Me with the baptism of fire. "I am used to pains, and trough The Spirit of GOD, I master my pains and the devil Satan is always in serious headaches when he tries me "for I always come out victorious" by the Spirit of the Lord Jesus-Christ who is always "with me." Matthew 4: 1-11

* I bless my Father Jesus Christ for his great love for me. Without the Lord Jesus Christ, I can no longer be alive "until now. What I am, is the grace , the mercy ", the love of God for me. The name" OF THE LORD JESUS CHRIST IS LIFE TO MY LUNGS, the name of the Lord Jesus Christ "is my Joyce" the name of the Lord Jesus Christ is my great power, "the name of the Lord Jesus Christ is my wealth", the name of the Lord Jesus Christ is my peace, "the name of the Lord Jesus Christ is my security," the name of the Lord Jesus Christ is the answer to my problems ***"THE NAME OF THE LORD JESUS CHRIST" IS LIFE OF AKINITENZAPA DIEUDONNE.***

**** SUFFERING WILL MAKE YOU A MAN AND MEN SHALL SAY TO YOU: - THIS IS THE MAN!***

*** *He who has not yet gone through fire "pray to God and say -
MY FATHER LET YOUR WILL BE DONE
IN MY LIFE. AMEN*!

* Sufferings made me to learn other things that I haven't heard from my father, DAD RICHARD N'KONJI. This is why it is very important to go through fire. "

However: - "I am a print of RICHARD N'KONJI"

-Honor your father! and GOD will honor you.

-Do not be a rebel to your fathers, but submit to them!

-Out of a lion, God can provide honey!

-Some times justice takes form of malice to bring justice!

-Pains calm pains

-call patience your father and it will give you the blessing of a father!

Listen to the words that prevent man in the wrong direction:

1. A good man calls his enemy at the table!
2. The smile of a soldier at war tells the win!
3. The one who needs to drink, drinks wine "and the one who needs to eat, eats bread!
4. Prayer of an orphan attracts the attention of God and of a widow grieves the heart of God and of a foreigner recalls the past to GOD!.
5. The one who writes 1, has also to learn to write one!
6. Love your husband, wife! That you may be saved!
7. The one who wants to live, eats his own body and drinks his own blood!
8. Let a patient be happy because he discovered the secret of healing!
9. Let the one who does not have breads, be happy, because he has the bread!

10 Let he who want to dress uses the model of God!
11. Let a pregnant woman be happy not because she has the child but because she is pregnant!
12. The cry of a son brings justice of a father!
13. The one who leaves himself to be slapped twice discovers the love of God!
14. It is through patience that justice comes!
15. Arrogance facilitates man to be trodden under foot of men! And humility attracts the hearts of men to a humble man!
16. Anger cry for those who loves innocence ! But peace shouts for one who loves condemnation!
17. Trough a father a child receives inheritance!
18 A trouble maker child buries his mother, and insults the efforts of his father!
19. Marriage makes man to feel enough, but children testify that he is married!

20. Blessed the one cannot give birth for a king will be born trough her!
21. Confidence eliminates the chances of failure!
22. He who loves women, is a friend to death!
23. Even a wise man loses his wisdom before a woman but the fear of God keeps man from the strange woman!
24. The one loves money is the prey of the devil, satan!
25. Do not watch the hand that is in the pocket of a man for many cry because of it!
26. The lips of a woman calm the anger of a king!
27. Close your eyes when a foreign woman is in front of you, because she seduces with her body!
28. A good meal always gives a man the desire to eat in his house!
29. He who eats with great appetite, encourages his wife to continue in the same style!

30. The One who wants to be one with God be one with her husband!
take care of what you did listen, and wisdom will be your friend!

Why God is against sorcery magic, fetishism, practice of prohibited?

A sorcerer, a magician, witchdoctor, one who practices the forbidden do not build love for one other. * The abominations are their food. "

God wants man to love his neighbor, forgive the fault of his neighbor, but a sorcerer uses the fault of a person * to enchant (curse)
* A sorcerer never like to see a happy couple, he seeks their mistakes to break into their home. * By the power he received from the devil satan, he creates desorder in houses by misunderstanding, infidelity, etc ...he is even able to remove the love of "husband for his wife and even of his children!

* A sorcerer can even give you an incurable disease. So when you're in the middle of a problem first examine your ways! When you see your sins, pray to your Father to forgive you in the name of the Lord Jesus Christ, and use the death "and resurrection of the Lord Jesus Christ" against the problem*:* ***USE THE BODY AND BLOOD OF THE LORD JESUS CHRIST!***

* A sorcerer can remove your result at school, university, to fail etc ... when he finds an open door into your life. When you reconciled with your father, apply the death * and * resurrection of the Lord Jesus Christ: ***USE THE BODY AND BLOOD OF THE LORD JESUS CHRIST.***

-* A sorcerer can bring the spirit of rebellion into the children, when man and woman are not one !...be one with your wife, your husband and the grace of God will cover your children "

-* A sorcerer can block your affairs when you do not live in peace with your wife, your husband!

-* A sorcerer can put mark of celibacy on you, in way when you have a fiance, you start to get sick, and this pushes man away to you. And after he walked away, you come back in good condition!

-* A sorcerer can put mark of failure on you to the point all you do never succeed!

-* A sorcerer can put mark of sterility on you so that you do not give birth to a child even when you get pregnant!

-* A sorcerer can put mark of death on you and just a headache and you die!

-* A sorcerer can put mark of loss, one nominate you today and tomorrow you're involved in accident and you lose the promotion!

-* A sorcerer can put in a person the spirit of fornication of fights- of lies *- disorder * -of adultery, etc. ....

a sorcerer feeds himself of human flesh and human blood *

God never gave human food for man! and the only food that God gives us is the Lord Jesus christ * *

A magician also operates as a sorcerer, He also feeds on human flesh and human blood * *

*ALL Those who feed on human flesh and human blood HAVE A PLACE TOGETHER WITH THE BEAST * *THE DRAGON, THE OTHER BEAST *PROSTITUTE, THE gods OF NATIONS in THE LAKE OF FIRE. REVELATION 20:10.*

LISTEN! Revelation 20:10: - and the devil that deceived them was cast into the lake of fire and brimstone where the beast and false prophet. They will be tormented day and night for ever and ever.

REVELATION 20: 15: - whosoever was not found written in the book of life was cast into the lake of fire.

* The witch doctors, practitioners are also involved in the table of demons and they operate also in hate * they also have part in the lake of fire * because they worship the devil and they have the mark of 666 , **THE NAME OF THE BEAST**.

Now that you are listing to the voice of the Lord Jesus Christ, renounce to magic *, to witchcraft * to fetishism, the practice banned to have a part with life to be judge for GOD to judge satan who retained you for long in bondage!

You know the devil, Satan asks you to do things that your conscience hate! however come to the Lord Jesus Christ, it is not too late, the Lord Jesus Christ will restore your life and he will restore your offspring and he will restore your person and your family ,the Lord Jesus Christ will restore all that you sacrificed to the devil *

***THE BLOOD OF THE LORD JESUS CHRIST REVIVED EVERYTHING Which IS DEAD ***

* Take your work tools, your books and bring them before the living God to be burned, and that you have share in the salvation that is in the **LORD JESUS CHRIST, THE ONLY SON OF THE LIVING GOD.**
* You who are sorcerer do not forget to cut your nail of work to be burned *. If your hair are snakes (scorpions) also cut them to be burned *- cut all the nails that you use them as a tool *

*The body and blood of the Lord Jesus christ will burn all things in your womb: * snakes, scorpions etc. and thou shalt be free from the devil, satan ***

My brother, my sister, according to everything you have read:

- who is good between God and satan ?

I, akini-dieudonne, i prefer God for his commandments are best and full of love .

my brother, my sister, i would like you to complete the sentence below!

*by supplementing it, you testify before God and satan, who is your master *. matthew 6:24*

I,..,I prefer..................for his commandments are best and full of love.

-how to raise a dead killed by sorcerers, magicians, witch doctors etc ...

listen to the teaching of the holy spirit:

-* Other deads are not dead under the will of God!
The devil Satan is in his court to convict men!

The devil, Satan does not want to be alone in the lake of fire with demons, he also wants men to be with him.

* Sorcerers, magicians, witch doctors, etc ... are the judges for the devil, Satan on Earth for their master has the power of death. they also have the power to kill anyone walking in disobedience to the living God.

*The work of those people, is to monitor all movements of men! they have remote controller, they place cameras *, microphones *, etc ... to record everything you do and said in order to build your case with reason to kill you * (- cameras - tmicros-phone etc ... can be webs, ants, cat,things you can not pay attention, etc ...)

LISTEN! I told you that the place of evil spirits are in unclean places! Is not it?

You know! These unclean insects , unclean reptiles, unclean birds , unclean animals, etc ... are homes of witches, * magicians * etc. ....

*** THE DEVIL, SATAN INCARNATED INTO A SNAKE TO GO TO MAN AND HIS WIFE TO KILL THEM!**

Similarly, those people, incarnate themself in unclean insects, unclean reptiles, unclean birds, unclean animals to go to people to kill them **SPIRITUALLY OR PHYSICALLY**!

* Have you ever seen a pig kill a child? (-Or insect-animals-reptiles cause death to men?)

* Parents who are not one * allow these people to destroy their children and their belongings!

LISTEN! By incarnation, they visit houses, and operate.

They can enchant your equipment or destroy them, they operate the way they want!

*- YOUR FEAR OF GOD IS A COVER OF YOUR CHILDREN!

LISTEN NOW! : - One who has received the Lord Jesus Christ and dies, he is not dead he sleeps!

-Other deads are dead, those who God himself strikes because of their abominations!

- Other deads are dead, those whom the devil, satan killed by his servants (magicians, sorcerers, witchdoctors, etc ...)
HEAR THE GOOD NEWS! THE BLOOD OF THE LORD JESUS CHRIST RISE UP THOSE THE DEVIL SATAN KILLS!

When these people kill, they keep the spirit of the person somewhere - on a tree! etc ...

*- When someone next to you died suddenly without a valid reason, do not start crying! lay your hand on him and begin to proclaim * the redemption of his spirit *
BY THE BLOOD OF THE LAMB OF GOD JESUS!

*- *have faith in the blood of the lamb of God Jesus pray untill he will return in life .* his spirit is just linked somewhere. "claim only the blood of the Lord Jesus christ the lamb of God and you will see the result!*

God always uses blood to save men from deadth. exodus 12: 1-13

-*I am not talking about something that i wish rather i did practised one day!*

I have already seen the blood of the Lord christ raise a dead by my hand!

LISTEN TO THE STORY! :-One night while we prayed in the living room, a little girl GEMIMA (3 years-4 years) left the room, and when I turned my eyes to her, I saw her felt on the ground and when I raced towards her, "her eyes was upward, fermented blood in his mouth and nose *, and his body was cold*. **SHE WAS HAVING LAST BEAT OF HEART!**
And I asked no one to panic (I was in charge that night,at the abscence of the Shepherd in charge). And I asked my brother SAMUEL-PHOBA, to carry the little GEMIMA. I ordered everyone to invoke God's fire to consume the sacrifice'altar. I said to my brother to invoke the **BLOOD OF THE LORD JESUS CHRIST**, and layed and kept my hand on her head. * After a few minutes the girl returned in her * and I quickly raced into the room where the girl was to take out 3 or 4 little witches who were there. We were preparing for their deliverance. We had woken up them, but one was not waked up. I moved the little boy, I have raised him, I have even hit on his head and was still sleeping, his body was like a dead, he felt absolutely nothing.

Another child say to me, he is out with a group of people to kill GEMIMA!

And I have ordered everyone to invoke fire on the group outside. I and man of God SAMUEL PHOBA invoked the blood of the Lord Jesus. My hand was also on his head and the little boy woke up from sleep.
We all went to the living room. The small GEMIMA spurred another crisis! -Fermented blood in her mouth and nose, eyes up, and we restarted the intercession at that time, the war was visible * bats invaded and flying all around the living room. The events since the first crisis of GEMIMA took a few hours of intercession and after 3 am, I told man of God SAMUEL PHOBA to take GEMIMA to hospital because the child had become pale and we went on foot, my hand still on her head, we walking to a clinic and the little GEMIMA was infused and restored to normal.

I do not know if the little GEMIMA can recognize that night, but at least her mom was there and his father was informed of this.

DO YOU BELIEVE NOW THAT THE BLOOD OF THE LORD JESUS CHRIST RAISES UP?

*- HOW TO PRAY!

- EX: - *gemima is dead!*

I claim the spirit of GEMIMA by the power of the Blood of the Lord Jesus Christ *, GEMIMA live by the power of the Blood of the Lord Jesus Christ.

NB: - repeat these words until the person returns alive.
- Talk wonders on the **BLOOD OF THE LORD JESUS CHRIST**.
- The prayer of faith will bring you to see the * resurrection.

Even after a few days, the resurrection is possible, because the Lord Jesus Christ lives in you .THE LORD JESUS raised up LAZARD after four days, and as he lives in you directly you have the power to raise up a dead after several days because the blood is already widely used, **THE BLOOD OF REDEMPTION, THE BLOOD OF THE LORD JESUS CHRIST *.**

Listen one more thing! the day of resurrection of the Lord Jesus Christ graves vomited people and they went to live in cities on earth!

<u>FIRE OF GOD</u>

It is by fire the devil, Satan will be judged, and us Christians, God has prepared us as judges to judge Satan and all his kingdom. However, we have the power to invoke fire of God over Satan, demons, etc ..

LISTEN: - fire is also a very effective weapon for those
That have God of Abraham, Isaac, and Jacob
FOR FATHER!

THIS IS HOW TO PRAY!:- By the authority that the Lord Jesus Christ gave me I invoke God's fire,
FIRE OF JUDGEMENT to come down as rain from the sky to anyone makes me war.

In my family, my work
At school, university etc ...
I invoke God's fire to consume the altar of sacrifice prepared for me by sorcerers (magicians witch doctors, etc.) to kill me.

NOTE: you will hear more details on the fire ***of God in the speech of akini:***
>
> ***"we are like***
> ***God for***
> ***knowledge of life"***

WHAT CAN A SORCERER (MAGICIAN, WITCHDOCTOR, THOSE WHO PRACTICE PROHIBITED) CAN DO TO REPARE THEIR RELATIONSHIP WITH GOD?

I beleive I have already answered to this question if you read at the beggining to this level. I have shown you that God is love, he also likes those people, and Us who have been already saved we have duty to love them.

THE LORD JESUS CHRIST SAID: - Love your enemies, bless them that curse you, do good to them that hate you, and pray for those who mistreat you and persecute you, that you may be the son of your father who is in heaven: for he makes his sun rise on the evil and the good, and sends rain on the just and the unjust. If you love those who love you, what reward have you? The pagans Publicains also do not act the same? And if you salute your brethren only, what do you do more? Pagans also act not the same way? Be perfect as your heavenly Father is perfect. Matthew 5: 44-48

He that have the mark to Perdition raises his eyes to the CROSS OF THE LORD JESUS CHRIST, so that THE BLOOD OF THE LORD JESUS CHRIST erases his sins and the mark of perdition 666 , the name of the beast.

* God's foolishness is wiser than men and the weakness of God is stronger than men! 1 COREINTHIENS 1: 17-25

Use your eyes to go to one that has the anointing *of GOD, SO THAT YOU MAY BE BLIND IN THE NAME OF THE LORD JESUS CHRIST, AND THE BODY AND BLOOD OF THE LORD JESUS CHRIST WILL OPEN YOUR EYES TO EAT FROM THE OTHER TREE: - THE TREE OF LIFE **

The body of the Lord Jesus christ and his blood are food that God gives man for ever and ever!

Do not fear the devil * satan * you shall not die if you agree to confess your sins because the Lord Jesus Christ himself will protect you against death (- against Satan *)

Do not forget that earth is the footstool of God, that is to say the Lord Jesus Christ walks on Satan and his kingdom!
May God who appeared to me into FIRE shows Himself by large signs in your life and all the earth in the name of his **ONLY SON THE LORD JESUS CHRIST. AMEN!**

This message is not a product of my imagination but rather a revelation from the Living God.

Please note: "We are like God for knowledge of life" is already published at www.createspace.com and availble on www.amazon.com market places.
Also note that "Sorcery(Magic)Made Man To Leave Eden" was first published by unibook or www.shopmybook.com and since the site went offline,you can no longer see the title.

www.ingramcontent.com/pod-product-compliance
Lightning Source LLC
Chambersburg PA
CBHW071358290426
44108CB00014B/1599